HOT SAUCE

HOT SAUCE

Fiery recipes for drizzling, dipping & marinating

Dan May

RYLAND PETERS & SMALL
LONDON • NEW YORK

Designer Paul Stradling
Editor Abi Waters
Head of Production Patricia Harrington
Creative Director Leslie Harrington
Editorial Director Julia Charles

Food Stylist Lizzie Harris
Prop Stylist Róisín Nield
Indexer Vanessa Bird

Published in 2025 by Ryland Peters & Small
20–21 Jockey's Fields
London WC1R 4BW
and
1452 Davis Bugg Road
Warrenton, NC 27589

www.rylandpeters.com

10 9 8 7 6 5 4 3 2 1

ISBN: 978-1-78879-685-9

A CIP record for this book is available from the
British Library.
US Library of Congress Cataloging-in-Publication
data has been applied for.

Printed and bound in China.

NOTES

• The recipes in this book are given in both metric
and imperial measurements. However, the spellings
are primarily British and this includes all terminology
relating to chilli peppers. British 'chilli' and 'chillies'
are used where Americans would use 'chile', 'chili'
and 'chiles'.

• The amount each recipe makes varies and is difficult
to estimate. Please refer to each recipe for storing
information and use as needed.

• All spoon measurements are level unless otherwise
specified.

• All herbs are fresh unless otherwise specified.

• All eggs are medium (UK) or large (US) unless
otherwise specified. Uncooked or partially cooked eggs
should not be served to the very young, the very old,
those with compromised immune systems, or to
pregnant women.

• When a recipe calls for the grated zest of citrus fruit,
buy unwaxed fruit and wash well before use. If you can
only find treated fruit, scrub well in warm soapy water
and rinse before using.

• Ovens should be preheated to the specified
temperature. Recipes in this book were tested using a
regular oven. If using a fan/convection oven, follow the
manufacturer's instructions for adjusting temperatures.

• Sterilize preserving jars before use. Wash them in hot,
soapy water and rinse in boiling water. Place in a large
saucepan and then cover with hot water. With the lid
on, bring the water to the boil and continue boiling for
15 minutes. Turn off the heat, then leave the jars in the
hot water until just before they are to be filled. Invert
the jars onto clean kitchen paper to dry. Sterilize the
lids for 5 minutes, by boiling, or according to the
manufacturer's instructions. Jars should be filled and
sealed while they are still hot.

MIX
Paper | Supporting
responsible forestry
FSC® C008047
www.fsc.org

CONTENTS

INTRODUCTION

Hot sauce is really having a moment! Its popularity is soaring, encouraging people to seek out not just the hottest sauces, but the tastiest and most unusual ones, too. This is in part due to its versatility as it can be enjoyed on all manner of foods from the predictable chicken wings, all the way through to using it to elevate an otherwise standard grilled cheese sandwich.

The beauty of this indispensable sauce is that it can come in many guises. Whether it be a classic chilli sauce using the hottest variety of chilli from Mexico, a rich curry paste full of depth from India, or even a sweet and spicy hot honey from the Mediterranean, the possibilities are really endless. With that in mind, I decided to take a tour of the culinary world and investigate the different sauces, marinades, pastes and rubs that can be found around the globe.

Many of the recipes in this book are ones I have, in principle, known for years and have loved to make but as I began to look at the ingredients and the way people cooked around the world I realized that each culture's approach to their food needed to be considered before I could really understand the processes and skills that make each recipe special. Each one is special because it represents a particular flavour combination or way of doing things that is often unique to a small geographic area. Although this book is undoubtedly about chillies and the love of chillies it is also about cooking, eating and sharing and how important these things are no matter where you happen to live.

Culturally it seems preparing fresh home-cooked meals is not regarded highly enough within our modern families to warrant the time or effort involved. It is interesting (or should I say impossible) to imagine say an Italian, Spanish or Greek family having no regard for the person who cooked for them or interest in the story of their food!

The most popular dishes of countries give us great insight into their culture. We readily accept and encourage change, which is probably what has kept our culture so alive and exciting over the past 150 years. There are few places in the world where chillies and spicy food have been so enthusiastically embraced or where the culture of eating chillies and challenging your palate reaches such extremes.

Despite the huge cultural differences between the Caribbean, the UK, Spain, South Africa, India, China, the USA and all the other regions covered in this book, there exists a unified 'chilli culture' that dares itself to eat hotter and hotter food, that loves to laugh at anyone who exceeds their tolerance and loves to share their food and experiences with anyone who is interested. There is fun and experimentation, and behind it all there is more often than not a willing social interaction, collaboration and good food!

So do we use cooking as an excuse to use spices and chillies or are they the excuse to cook? I don't think it really matters; as long as the two go hand in hand we get the fun and the benefits of both; as well as hopefully preserving some pretty fantastic old recipes and learning how to use them.

Challenge yourself to discover and experiment with the recipes in this collection and jump on the hot sauce bandwagon to take your cooking to new levels.

1
MEXICO & SOUTH AMERICA

NOTED CHILLIES

The Poblano which, when ripened fully and dried, is referred to as the Ancho, Chipotle, Orange Habanero, Rocoto, Pasilla, Brazilian Starfish, Aji Amarillo (pictured opposite), Aji Limo.

CHILLI FACTS & FICTION

Aztec kings used to drink a combination of hot chocolate and crushed dried chillies to 'stimulate' themselves before visiting their concubines.

ROAST TOMATO & CHIPOTLE HOT SAUCE

This is another absolute classic from Mexico with loads of variations, but I like the way this one balances the smokiness of the Chipotle chillies with the sweetness of the onion and tomatoes.

5–6 Chipotle chillies

400 g/14 oz. vine-ripened tomatoes (the riper the better), halved

2 fresh bay leaves

2 thyme sprigs

2 tbsp olive oil

1 large onion, roughly chopped

3–4 garlic cloves, roughly chopped

1 small glass of red wine

2 tbsp agave syrup

1 tsp mustard powder

1 tsp dried oregano

sea salt and black pepper

Put the chillies in a bowl, add a little warm water and leave to soak for about 20–30 minutes.

Preheat the oven to 190°C (375°F) Gas 5.

Put the tomatoes in a roasting pan with the bay leaves and thyme. Drizzle with most of the oil and sprinkle with a little salt. Roast in the preheated oven until the tomatoes are starting to brown – 45–50 minutes. Remove from the oven and leave to cool a little.

Heat the remaining oil in a small frying pan/skillet. Fry the onion gently until it begins to turn golden, add the garlic and fry for a further 3–4 minutes. Add the wine and allow to cook for a further few minutes to steam off the alcohol. Remove from the heat.

Take the chillies from the water, remove their stems and deseed them. Put in a food processor or blender with the onion, garlic and wine mixture. Remove the skins from the roasted tomatoes and add the flesh to the food processor. Blend everything together to a smooth paste.

Transfer the paste to a small saucepan with the agave syrup, mustard and oregano and mix thoroughly. Heat over medium heat to a gentle simmer, stirring regularly. Reduce the heat and allow to cook for a further 10 minutes until the sauce reduces to your desired consistency. Taste and season with salt and pepper as required.

The sauce will keep for several weeks in an airtight container in the fridge.

Hot tip: Use this with a full English (cooked) breakfast or in a chicken or sausage sandwich for great results!

YUCATECAN ACHIOTE PASTE (RECADO ROJO)

Yucatán is the traditional home to the Mayan people, and their influence (along with that of Spanish and Caribbean cuisine) is very apparent in local dishes, creating very diverse results.

2 tbsp annatto seeds

1 tbsp black peppercorns

5–6 allspice berries

2 tsp cumin seeds

2 tsp Mexican wild oregano

2 tsp sea salt

1 tsp ground cinnamon

8 garlic cloves, crushed

½ tsp finely chopped Habanero chilli

60 ml/¼ cup sour orange juice, or 1 tbsp orange juice and 3 tbsp lime juice

Put the annatto, peppercorns, allspice, cumin, oregano and salt in a heavy-duty mortar and grind together with a pestle. Annatto seeds are very hard, so the heavier the grinding implement the easier it will be. You can always use a coffee or spice grinder.

When you have achieved a fairly fine grind, add the cinnamon, garlic and chilli and continue grinding. Add the orange juice and pound to a smooth paste. Cover and refrigerate until ready to use.

The paste will keep for several months in an airtight container in the fridge.

Hot tip: Use this with pork, turkey, rice and fish

MOLE POBLANO

4 Guajillo chillies, deseeded and roughly torn

6 Ancho chillies, deseeded and roughly torn

3 Pasilla chillies, deseeded and roughly torn

3-cm/1¼-inch piece cinnamon stick, roughly broken

½ piece star anise

¼ tsp coriander seeds

3 cloves

1 tsp sesame seeds

8 black peppercorns

¼ tsp dried marjoram

½ tsp Mexican wild oregano

a large pinch of dried thyme

½ onion, quartered

10 garlic cloves, skin on

200 g/7 oz. tomatillos

120 g/4½ oz. ripe tomatoes

1 tbsp vegetable oil

50 g/⅓ cup almonds

30 g/1 oz. walnuts

20 g/¾ oz. peanuts

2 tbsp pumpkin seeds

½ small corn tortilla, torn into small pieces

50 g/⅓ cup raisins

500 ml/2 cups chicken stock, warmed

50 g/2 oz. Mexican chocolate, broken into pieces

sea salt and ground white pepper

Mole Poblano has reached a status so legendary that it is easy to be afraid to even attempt making one! It is yet another recipe that has no shortcuts and requires a degree of devotion to complete. Delicious and immensely satisfying, once you have made it from scratch, you will not only feel very smug but you will also see just how poor storebought 'moles' can be. Mole Poblano is perhaps the best way of using up leftover turkey and chicken.

Put the chillies in a heavy-based frying pan/skillet and dry-roast them until they begin to char slightly. Remove from the heat immediately. Put the chillies in a bowl, add a little hot water and allow to soak for 20–30 minutes. Drain and reserve the soaking liquid.

In the same pan, toast the cinnamon, star anise, coriander, cloves, sesame seeds and peppercorns over medium heat until they begin to brown and release their aromas. Pour into a bowl and allow to cool. Grind in a coffee or spice grinder until fine. Mix with the herbs and set aside.

Preheat a grill/broiler. Put the onion, garlic, tomatillos and tomatoes in a roasting pan under the hot grill/broiler and toast, turning frequently, until each ingredient is beginning to lightly char. You may want to do this in batches of like ingredients. Allow to cool, then peel the garlic.

In the same heavy-based pan, heat the oil over medium heat and fry the nuts, pumpkin seeds and tortilla pieces until they are well coloured but not burnt. Warning: pumpkin seeds pop as they are fried, so cover the pan with a mesh lid, if you like. Remove from the heat and lift out the nuts, seeds and tortilla pieces from the oil using a slotted spoon. Set the pan and the oil aside.

Put the nuts, seeds, tortilla pieces, raisins and charred onion, garlic, tomatillos and tomatoes in a food processor. Blend until you have a smooth paste, adding the stock as required. Remove the stems from the soaked chillies and add the flesh to the food processor. Blend until they are completely broken down into the paste. Add the ground, roasted spices and blend again. Add some of the chilli soaking liquid and/or stock, if required, as you blend.

Return the reserved pan with its oil to the heat and gently reheat. Force the paste through a fine sieve/strainer into the pan with the back of a spoon to remove any remaining gritty bits. Bring it to a very gentle simmer and simmer over very low heat (and I mean really low!), adding stock as required, for about 60–75 minutes. Stir very regularly. You can cover it, but I tend to leave it uncovered and add stock as required.

Season with salt and add the chocolate. Cook for about 10–15 minutes, stirring to ensure the chocolate has melted. Add salt and some white pepper to taste.

Hot tip: Use with lightly poached chicken or turkey served with basmati rice, or in a tortilla (as a taco) sprinkled with toasted sesame seeds.

AJÍ AMARILLO SAUCE

This ubiquitous Peruvian chilli sauce can be made with Jalapeño chillies, but there is nothing quite like the real thing made with the famous yellow chillies of Peru.

250 g/9 oz. Ají Amarillo chillies
(or Jalapeños), halved and deseeded

1 roasted garlic clove

2 tsp sugar

2 tsp lime juice

1 tsp cider vinegar

2 tbsp olive oil

sea salt

Put the chillies and a little water in a saucepan, bring to a gentle simmer and cook for 10 minutes. Add the garlic, sugar, lime juice and vinegar and continue to simmer, stirring regularly to dissolve the sugar. Add a good pinch of salt. Blend to a smooth paste with a stick blender or in a food processor. Gradually add the oil while blending, until the desired consistency is reached. Add more salt if required, and allow to cool.

The sauce will keep for several weeks in an airtight container in the fridge.

Hot tip: Use with anything – but it is particularly good with seafood or potato dishes.

CHIMICHURRI

Chimichurri is a herby, garlicky concoction that works equally well as an accompanying sauce or as a marinade. It rarely features much chilli but the addition of a Jalapeño provides some warmth.

1 small shallot, very finely chopped

1 green Jalapeño chilli, deseeded and finely chopped

juice of 1 small lime

a large handful of flat-leaf parsley, finely chopped

3 tbsp sherry vinegar or red wine vinegar

4 large garlic cloves, crushed

2 tsp dried oregano or
2 tbsp fresh oregano

1 fresh bay leaf, finely chopped and woody stem removed

1 tsp red and green peppercorns, freshly ground

125 ml/½ cup extra virgin olive oil

½ tsp sea salt

Put the shallot, chilli and lime juice in a small bowl and mix well. Cover and set aside for about 1 hour.

Combine the remaining ingredients in a separate bowl and stir together. Add the shallot mixture and mix thoroughly. This sauce can also be made equally well by giving the ingredients a couple of pulses in a food processor. Cover and allow the flavours to mingle until required.

The acidic nature of this blend allows it to store well for several weeks in an airtight container in the fridge.

Hot tip: Use as a marinade for strips of beef or chicken, or with lamb or fish.

BOLIVIAN LLAJUA HOT SAUCE

This sauce is made using Rocoto peppers, or Locoto as they are known in Bolivia. They are odd chilli plants from the species *Capsicum pubescens*, and their leaves and stems are covered in tiny hairs. Unusually, they are able to withstand cooler temperatures than other species producing a similar heat. We have used a combination of coriander/cilantro and basil in this sauce to replicate the flavour of quilquiña – Bolivian coriander.

3–4 large vine-ripened tomatoes, halved and deseeded

1 red Rocoto chilli (or red Habanero), deseeded

2 plump garlic cloves, roughly chopped

a small handful of coriander/cilantro

about 10 basil leaves

olive oil, as required

½ tsp sea salt, or to taste

Put all the ingredients, except the oil and salt, into a food processor/blender and pulse until you have a coarse paste. Add oil to aid blending and to achieve the required consistency. Taste and season with salt.

Hot tip: Use as a fresh salsa for barbecued pork or chicken, or with grilled/broiled chicken.

PEBRE

Perhaps the most commonly served sauce in Chile, Pebre is served with most cooked meats and varies greatly in its constituent parts. The recipe below is a good starting point, but feel free to experiment. Make it a few hours in advance, as the flavours improve as they mingle.

2 tbsp olive oil

1 tbsp red wine vinegar

100 ml/scant ½ cup water

4–5 fresh Aji chillies (Aji Limo work brilliantly), finely chopped

2 garlic cloves

1 small onion, finely chopped

a large handful of coriander/cilantro, finely chopped

1 tbsp oregano, finely chopped

½ tsp salt

In a medium bowl, beat the oil, vinegar and water together. Add the remaining ingredients and mix thoroughly together.

It can be kept for a few days in an airtight container in the fridge.

Hot tip: Use with barbecued meats.

AJÍ DE HUACATAY

Here is a very simple version of a sauce that is common throughout Bolivia and Peru. Regular additions to this recipe would be milk (even condensed milk) and/or cotija cheese – a close relative of feta that is salty and crumbly but made with cow's milk. The addition of the cheese makes this sauce delicious when poured over steamed new potatoes. I would use about 50 g/ 1½ oz. of feta cheese, crumbled and blended with the chillies and herbs, before the oil is added.

1 Rocoto chilli (or Habanero), finely chopped

1 Ají Amarillo chilli (or Jalapeño), finely chopped

a small bunch of huacatay (*Tagetes minuta* – black mint/ Amazonian mint), or garden mint leaves

a few quilquiña leaves (*Porophyllum ruderale* – Bolivian coriander), or coriander/cilantro, finely chopped

½ celery stick, roughly chopped

about 100 ml/scant ½ cup sunflower oil

sea salt and black pepper

Mix together the chillies, herbs and celery. Add enough oil to produce a slick salsa. Season with salt and pepper to taste.

Hot tip: Use with potato dishes and poached meats.

CLASSIC GUACAMOLE

(opposite, top)

If you want a classic dip with a long history, then look no further than guacamole – originally made by the Aztecs in the 16th century. In its purest form, all it contains is avocado mashed with salt, but more and more variations have been developed over the centuries. This is my favourite version.

3 ripe avocados, skinned, pitted and roughly chopped

1 vine-ripened tomato, skinned, deseeded and roughly chopped

3 fresh green chillies, deseeded and finely chopped

juice of 2 small limes

a little extra virgin olive oil

2 spring onions/scallions, finely chopped

a small bunch of coriander/ cilantro, finely chopped

sea salt and black pepper

In a large bowl, mash the avocados, tomato and chillies together with the lime juice. The consistency should be chunky yet smooth – add a little olive oil to help achieve this. Add the onions and coriander and mix well. Season with salt and pepper to taste and serve immediately.

Hot tip: Use with tortillas to dip, on nachos, on the side of a spicy chilli, or in homemade burritos.

SALSA ROJA *(opposite, bottom)*

If you can't get fresh De Arbol and Guajillo, use dried, toast them for 2 minutes on each side, soak in a small amount of boiling water for about 20 minutes, then remove their stems and deseed them, reserving the soaking liquid.

2 tbsp olive oil

1 onion, finely chopped

4–5 large plum tomatoes, halved and core removed

2–3 garlic cloves

1 tsp dried oregano

1 fresh Serrano or Jalapeño chilli, deseeded and chopped

3 fresh or dried De Arbol chillies, deseeded and chopped

5 fresh or dried Guajillo chillies, deseeded and chopped

a small bunch of coriander/ cilantro, finely chopped

sea salt and black pepper

Heat a heavy-based frying pan/skillet or griddle over fairly high heat. Add a little oil and fry the onion and tomatoes hard for 7–11 minutes until they begin to blacken, but stir as required to prevent burning. Add the garlic and cook for a further 3–4 minutes.

Transfer the contents of the pan to a food processor with the oregano and chillies. Add the remaining oil as you blend (and the liquid you soaked the chillies in, if you used dried) until you have a smooth and even paste. Season to taste with salt and pepper, then add the coriander and briefly blend again to mix through.

Place into a tightly sealed jar and allow to cool. The flavours will improve over the next few days if you can wait that long! Serve at room temperature.

The salsa will keep for 1–2 weeks, refrigerated.

Hot tip: Use to spice up sandwiches, sausages and burgers, with nachos or tacos, or in burritos.

2
AFRICA

NOTED CHILLIES

Fatali Habanero (pictured opposite, right), Malawian Kambuzi,
African Bird's Eye (Peri-Peri – pictured opposite, left).

CHILLI FACTS & FICTION

In West Africa, crushed chillies are mixed with fresh lime juice and used
as an enema. Unsurprisingly, this is guaranteed to cure constipation.

MOROCCAN TAGINE PASTE

Slow cooking requires little effort to get a rich flavour and tenderly cooked food. The basis for all pastes is to get the aromatics and flavourings out of the spices and infused into the wet ingredients.

1 tbsp sunflower oil

1 onion, roughly chopped

1 sweet/bell red pepper, chopped

5–6 garlic cloves, crushed

1–2 tbsp Jordanian Baharat Blend (see page 68)

200 g/1⅔ cups passata (Italian sieved tomatoes)

100 g/⅔ cup chickpeas/garbanzo beans (drained weight)

50 g/⅓ cup ready-to-eat dried apricots, chopped

50 g/⅓ cup dried dates, chopped

3-cm/1¼-inch piece fresh ginger, peeled and finely chopped

zest and juice of 1 lemon

1 tsp tomato purée/paste

1 tbsp cider vinegar

1 tsp sugar

1 tsp sea salt, or to taste

Heat the oil in a heavy-based saucepan over medium heat. Add the onion and cook for 2–3 minutes. Add the red pepper and garlic and fry for 3 minutes. Stir in My Favourite Jordanian Baharat Blend, then add the remaining ingredients and heat to a gentle simmer. Cook, stirring regularly, for 5 minutes.

Remove the pan from the heat and blend well with a stick blender or food processor until it forms a glossy, thick and smooth paste. If you feel it is a little dry, add water 1 teaspoon at a time and return it to the heat to heat through. If the mixture is too loose, return to it to the heat and simmer for a few minutes more to cook off some of the excess moisture.

When you are happy with the consistency, spoon the paste into a sterilized jar and seal tightly. Store in the fridge until needed. The paste will continue to improve over a couple of weeks.

The paste should keep for many months in a sealed, sterilized container. Once opened, store in the fridge and use within 4 weeks.

Hot tip: This paste is perfect for flavouring slow-cooked North African and Middle Eastern stews. Use with lamb, mushrooms, squash and salmon.

CHERMOULA

A delicious marinade with a robust yet light flavour, chermoula is popular along the entire coastal region of North West Africa where there is almost an infinite number of variations.

2 tsp cider vinegar or white wine vinegar

a few saffron threads

a bunch of coriander/cilantro, finely chopped

a small bunch of flat-leaf parsley, finely chopped

4 garlic cloves, crushed

1 red chilli, deseeded and finely chopped

2 tbsp paprika

1 tbsp ground cumin

1 tsp sea salt

½ tsp cayenne pepper

juice of 1 lemon

2–3 tbsp olive oil

Heat the vinegar in a very small saucepan and add the saffron. Remove from the heat and allow to cool.

In a medium bowl mix together the coriander, parsley, garlic and chilli. Add the other dry ingredients and mix well.

Pour in the lemon juice, oil and the vinegar and saffron mixture. Stir very well together, then cover the sauce until you are ready to use it. If you do not intend to use immediately, transfer the mixture to a jar, seal tightly and store in the fridge. This blend is best used fresh.

Hot tip: Use this to stuff sardines or mackerel before they are grilled/broiled or barbecued. Delicious with roasted veg.

HARISSA PASTE

In many ways Harissa is the taste of North Africa. It is commonly associated with Tunisia, but you can find variations throughout Morocco, Algeria and Libya. These include adding caramelized shallots or fresh rose petals, resulting in the famous rose Harissa. It can add a great little fiery kick to any dish and is an essential addition to *lablabi*, the Tunisian breakfast soup made with chickpeas, garlic and egg.

50 g/1¾ oz. dried chilli/hot red pepper flakes, preferably Bakloutis

1 tsp cumin seeds

1 tsp coriander seeds

1 tsp caraway seeds, freshly ground

1 red sweet/bell pepper, roasted, skinned and deseeded

1 tsp sea salt

4 garlic cloves, chopped

1 tsp smoked paprika

1 tbsp red wine vinegar

2 tbsps tomato purée/paste

finely grated zest and juice from ½ a lemon

½ preserved lemon, finely chopped

good-quality olive oil, if needed (see method)

Put the dried chilli flakes in a bowl and cover with a little hot water (DO NOT BREATHE IN THE FUMES!). Cover and leave for 15–20 minutes to rehydrate. Meanwhile, put the cumin, coriander and caraway seeds in a dry skillet and toast over medium heat.

Drain the water from the dried chilli flakes and put the flakes into a food processor. Add the toasted spices and the remaining ingredients except the oil. Blend until you have a smooth paste. Add a little olive oil to the paste while blending, if required, to achieve a smooth consistency. Tip into a small saucepan and heat gently until just bubbling. Add a little water, if required, to prevent burning, and simmer gently for 10 minutes.

Transfer to a small sterilized jar and top up with olive oil, ensuring the paste is completely covered. Seal tightly and store in the fridge for up to 4 months. It is a good idea to top up the jar with olive oil each time you use some of the paste to make sure it is not exposed to the air. This will greatly help improve the length of time you can store your harissa.

Hot tip: Use this as the base for a marinade for fish or chicken or add a spoonful to a tagine or other spicy stew.

THE ULTIMATE PERI-PERI MARINADE

The story of Peri-Peri (or Piri-Piri, or Pili-Pili) in all its forms encapsulates the story of chillies and their spread across the world over the last 400 years. Piri-Piri itself simply means 'chilli chilli' in the dialect of southern Mozambique and it generally refers to the African Bird's Eye. It is most likely to have been introduced to these regions by the Portuguese (who are also responsible for introducing chillies to India); they had in turn brought the spice over from the Americas. Today, we refer to Peri-Peri as the marinade or sauce that, although likely to be Portuguese in origin, is most closely associated with its former colonies of Mozambique and Angola. This is my take on a classic recipe. As with all marinades of this kind it benefits from a little ageing before being pressed into service. I would recommend making this a couple of days before you need it, and storing it in a jar in the fridge, giving it a little shake a couple of times a day!

2 tsp nut oil

3 limes, quartered

1 large onion, very finely chopped

10 red Bird's Eye chillies (or 5 Bird's Eye and 2 Fatali), deseeded and finely chopped

1 garlic bulb, cloves crushed

zest of 1 lemon and juice of 2 lemons

a large bunch of flat-leaf parsley, finely chopped

2 fresh bay leaves, central stalk discarded, finely chopped

180 ml/scant ¾ cup olive oil

100 ml/scant ½ cup cider vinegar

2 tbsp sea salt

½ tsp smoked paprika

3 tbsp sweet paprika

1 tsp dried oregano

Heat a frying pan/skillet over medium heat and add the nut oil. Fry each cut side of the limes until they start to develop a good colour; it can help to gently press the limes onto the pan with the back of a fork, as this releases a little more of the juice and aids the caramelization of the sugars. Remove from the pan and set aside with any juice in the pan.

Put the onion, chillies and garlic in a large bowl and squeeze into this the juice from the caramelized limes. Add the lemon zest and fresh juice. Add the parsley and bay leaves and mix thoroughly.

Pour the olive oil into a separate bowl and add the vinegar, salt, smoked and sweet paprika and oregano. Whisk together to combine.

Add to the chilli mixture and stir thoroughly to combine well. Pour into a glass jar and seal. Put in the fridge and leave to mature for at least 24 hours, but preferably 48 hours, giving the jar a regular shake. Use within 4–5 days.

Hot tip: Use this as a marinade for chicken, beef or prawns/shrimp or as a dip for these and for spicy sausages.

LA KAMA SPICE BLEND

The cubeb berries used in this recipe are the precursor to the black and white pepper we use today. Although not strictly chilli, La Kama is a deliciously light and peppery seasoning from Tangier.

2 tsp cubeb berries
1 tbsp ground ginger
1 tbsp ground turmeric
1 tbsp ground black pepper
2 tsp ground cinnamon
1 tsp grated nutmeg

Put the chillies and a little water in a saucepan, bring to a gentle simmer and cook for 10 minutes. Add the garlic, sugar, lime juice and vinegar and continue to simmer, stirring regularly to dissolve the sugar. Add a good pinch of salt. Blend to a smooth paste with a stick blender or in a food processor. Gradually add the oil while blending, until the desired consistency is reached. Add more salt if required, and allow to cool. The sauce will keep for several weeks in an airtight container in the fridge.

Hot tip: Use on chicken, fish or veg, or even to flavour a pan of lentils or couscous. Try combining it with a little lemon zest as a marinade for chicken or adding a little cumin and rolling a lamb joint in it before roasting.

RAS EL HANOUT SPICE BLEND

2 tsp ground cumin
2 tsp ground turmeric
2 tsp ground ginger
2 tsp sea salt
2 tsp brown sugar
1 tsp ground black pepper
1 tsp ground cinnamon
1 tsp ground coriander
1 tsp cayenne pepper
1 tsp ground allspice
1 tsp ground fennel seeds
1 tsp blue poppy seeds
½ tsp ground cardamom
½ tsp ground cloves
½ tsp dried rose petals, ground,
or dried culinary lavender flowers

This is a simple version of a legendary spice blend. Meaning 'top of the store' in Arabic, or more often 'house blend', it can contain anything up to 50–60 ingredients. It is also a key constituent in the Classic North African Rub recipe (see page 39).

Put all the ingredients in a large bowl and mix thoroughly. Store in a tightly sealed jar in a cool, dark place, until required.

Hot tip: It has so many uses, but I would definitely recommend trying it in a slow-cooked rabbit casserole, with poached or scrambled eggs and as flavouring when cooking lentils.

CLASSIC SOUTH AFRICAN BRAII SAUCE

Braii is the Afrikaans word for 'barbecue' and is perhaps the defining cooking method in South African food. Braiis are universally wood-fired and are literally everywhere. It is a method and approach to barbecuing I have taken to heart and recommend to everyone! This is a fantastic recipe (from Paarl) for a sauce to be used as a marinade or table sauce; however, it really comes into its own as a fabulous baste for meat while it is being barbecued. The chillies are added to taste and there can be anything from none up to a good handful!

1 large onion, roughly chopped

4 garlic cloves, roughly chopped

1 red sweet/bell pepper, deseeded and chopped

2–3 Bird's Eye chillies, deseeded and chopped

3 tbsp red wine vinegar

about 1 tbsp olive oil

400-g/14-oz. can plum tomatoes, drained

1 tbsp tomato purée/paste

2 tbsp Worcestershire sauce

2 tbsp homemade fruity chutney

1 tsp cayenne pepper

3–4 tbsp muscovado/molasses sugar

1 tsp mustard powder

Put all the ingredients into a blender or food processor and pulse until you have a smooth, glossy paste. Loosen with a little more oil or water if required. Store in an airtight jar in the fridge until you are ready to use. This recipe benefits from being made a little in advance – a day or two is ideal!

Hot tip: Use this with all meats, or even spicy sausage. It makes an excellent marinade for game birds too – try this with pheasant breast.

PINANG KERRIE SAUCE

The Cape Malay cooking of southern South Africa results in some of the best spicy food in the world. This recipe shows a simple blending of styles and creates the perfect flavouring for a 'hot' lamb curry.

1 tbsp Malay Curry Powder
(see page 111)

1 tsp ground turmeric

1 tsp sea salt

1 tsp palm sugar

2 tbsp cider vinegar

1 tsp tamarind paste

1 tbsp dark soy sauce

2.5-cm/1-inch piece fresh ginger,
peeled and grated

4–5 garlic cloves, crushed

3 Zimbabwe Bird (or Bird's Eye)
chillies

1 tbsp sunflower oil

2 bay leaves

2 tbsp coriander/cilantro
stalks and leaves,
chopped

Put all the ingredients in a blender or food processor and pulse until you have a smooth, thick paste. Add a little water if the consistency is too thick. Store in an airtight container until ready to use. The flavours will improve if made a couple of days in advance.

Hot tip: Use this to cook with lamb, pork and chicken.

ETHIOPIAN BERBERE PASTE

Berbere may sound exotic, but it simply means 'hot' in the Amharic language of Ethiopia. It is used both in cooking (a requirement for Dabo Kolo – a traditional crunchy bread snack) and as an accompaniment for almost any meat, vegetable or rice dish.

1 tsp cardamom pods

5–6 cloves

½ tsp coriander seeds

½ tsp cumin seeds

1½ tsp fenugreek seeds

2 tbsp dried chilli/hot red pepper flakes

2 tbsp paprika

1 tbsp sea salt

½ tsp black peppercorns, coarsely ground

½ tsp ground turmeric

¼ tsp ground allspice

a good grating of nutmeg

a good pinch of ground cinnamon

1 large onion, finely chopped

5-cm/2-inch piece fresh ginger, peeled and finely chopped

4 garlic cloves, crushed

2 tbsp deseeded and finely chopped Habanero chillies

about 4 tbsp groundnut oil

Put the cardamom pods in a small saucepan and add the cloves, coriander, cumin and fenugreek. Toast over medium heat, keeping the spices moving to avoid charring them. Remove from the heat.

When cool enough to handle, take the cardamom seeds out of the pods and put these into a food processor or mortar with the other toasted spices. Add the other dry ingredients and pulse repeatedly, or grind with a pestle, to create a fairly coarse but even powder – or to your preferred consistency.

Add the onion, ginger, garlic and fresh chillies, and blend or grind again. Add the oil while blending to alter the consistency. The final Berbere should be smooth, thick and glossy without being sticky.

Hot tip: Use this added to any type of stew or as a REALLY spicy table dip.

NITER KIBBEH

¼ tsp fenugreek seeds

1–2-cm/½–¾-inch piece cinnamon
stick, roughly broken up

1–2 cloves

1 small hot dried chilli, deseeded

¼ tsp cardamom seeds

½ tsp ground turmeric

a generous pinch of grated nutmeg

250 g/2 sticks unsalted butter, cut
into chunks

1 shallot (or small onion), very finely
chopped

2 garlic cloves, very finely chopped

2.5-cm/1-inch piece fresh ginger,
peeled and finely grated

This spiced clarified butter, a staple of Ethiopian cuisine, is a
great addition to any storecupboard, as it keeps for longer than
conventional butter and can be used to cook at higher temperatures
without burning. It is similar to the ghee used in Indian cooking,
but the addition of the spices makes it far more flavoursome.

Put the fenugreek in a heavy-based saucepan with the cinnamon, cloves,
chilli and cardamom seeds. Toast until they begin to release their aroma.
Remove from the pan and grind to a fine powder in a spice grinder or using
a mortar and pestle. Stir in the turmeric and nutmeg.

Melt the pieces of butter in the pan over gentle heat, stirring regularly to
ensure they don't catch on the pan. Turn the heat up and bring the butter to
a boil. Add the shallot, garlic and ginger and fry for 2 minutes, then stir in the
ground spice mixture. Make sure everything is evenly mixed, because the
mixture must not be stirred again during cooking. Reduce the heat and cook
at a very gentle simmer for 50 minutes.

A clear 'butter' should float to the surface. Strain this liquid through a muslin
into a second pan to remove all the butter solids and spices. Repeat if
necessary to obtain a completely clear liquid.

Pour into a sterilized jar, seal and store in the fridge. The liquid
will turn solid as it chills and will keep for several months
in the fridge.

Hot tip: Use this to make fantastically flavoursome
cheese scones, in scrambled eggs or in the place
of ghee in Indian curries.

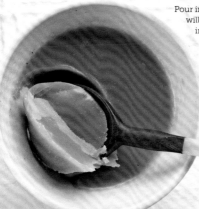

EGUSI SAUCE *(opposite, left)*

Egusi is commonly found in West Africa as a soup, but in Central and East Africa it is far more commonly used as a sauce. It is traditionally thickened using flour made from the seeds of the squash family. Pumpkin seeds are readily available and are great for making this delicious, high-protein sauce for grilled/broiled meats, rice or vegetables. To prepare the pumpkin seeds for this recipe, roast them on a baking tray at 180°C (350°F) Gas 4 until they begin to colour; you may need to turn them to aid even cooking. Allow them to cool and then blitz to a fine powder in a food processor.

2 tbsp vegetable oil

1 large onion, finely chopped

2 large tomatoes, chopped

1 red sweet/bell pepper, finely chopped

1 Fatali Habanero chilli, (or any Habanero or hot chilli), stalk removed

225 g/1¾ cups pumpkin seed flour (or egusi)

sea salt and black pepper

Heat the oil in a saucepan over medium heat and fry the onion for 5 minutes. Add the tomatoes, sweet/bell pepper and chilli. Mix together, then cover and cook for 10 minutes, stirring occasionally.

Stir in the flour and mix thoroughly. Add water as required to create a smooth sauce; you can use a stick blender to pulse the sauce to get an even and smooth consistency, if you like. bring to a gentle simmer. Cook for 3–5 minutes until thickened. Season with salt and pepper, and serve.

Hot tip: Use this to accompany plain rice and grilled/broiled meats.

PILI-PILI SAUCE *(opposite, right)*

Ubiquitous throughout tropical Africa, Pili-Pili can be found in one form or another. This recipe comes from East Africa and was one of the first recipes I tried when I first began making chilli sauces. It eventually evolved into the all-purpose African Hot Sauce that we now make. This purist version has no onion and no tomatoes or sweet peppers – just a lot of chillies, lemon and garlic. Used as a dipping sauce throughout the region it is certainly not for the faint-hearted.

100 g/3½ oz. Fatali Habanero chillies (or other hot chillies), stalks removed

3 garlic cloves, roughly chopped

juice of 1 lemon

a small handful of roughly chopped mixed herbs (such as parsley, coriander/cilantro and oregano)

2 tbsp vegetable oil

sea salt

Put all the ingredients in a food processor and pulse until you have a coarse but well mixed sauce. Add a little water to aid mixing, if required. (To make using a mortar and pestle, first grind the chillies and garlic with some salt, then add the herbs, lemon juice and oil.)

Cook the blended mixture in a frying pan/skillet over medium-high heat for 2 minutes, or until the garlic is softened, then pour into a sterilized container to cool. Seal until airtight. This will store well in the fridge for weeks and probably months!

Hot tip: Use this with anything that needs a touch of fire!

TSIRE POWDER

A wonderfully simple West African spice blend, Tsire Powder is ideal for adding a delicious seasoning and a tasty bit of crunch to meat kebabs/kabobs. It is also excellent when sprinkled over roasting vegetables or even salads. If you like, make a larger batch – it stores well.

100 g/3½ oz. salted roasted peanuts
2 tsp chilli powder
½ tsp grated nutmeg
½ tsp ground ginger
½ tsp ground cinnamon
¼ tsp ground cloves
¼ tsp ground allspice

Grind the peanuts into a coarse powder using a grinder or a mortar and pestle. Tip into a bowl and stir in the other ingredients, ensuring everything is evenly blended. Pour into an airtight container, seal and store in a cool, dark place until required.

Hot tip: Use this to coat chicken before frying, or add a spoonful or two to a homemade burger mix for extra flavour and texture.

CLASSIC NORTH AFRICAN RUB

This robust seasoned rub makes good use of the Ras el Hanout dry spice blend. It is has a deliciously intense flavour, which works particularly well if combined with a little yogurt to make a simple marinade.

2 tbsp sea salt

3 tsp caraway seeds

2 tsp dried oregano

1 tsp cumin seeds

1 tsp dried rosemary

½ tsp dried chilli/hot red pepper flakes

3 tsp Ras el Hanout Spice Blend (see page 31)

1 tsp ground turmeric

5 garlic cloves, roasted in their skins for 15 minutes, or until soft

3–4 tbsp olive oil

Grind the salt, caraway, oregano, cumin, rosemary and chilli flakes together to create a fine powder, either using a spice grinder or a mortar and pestle. Tip into a bowl and stir in the Ras el Hanout Spice Blend and turmeric.

Squeeze out the soft roasted garlic flesh into the bowl and add enough olive oil to make a smooth paste. Combine all the ingredients thoroughly.

This mixture will keep well if put into a small sterilized jar and topped up with olive oil.

Hot tip: Use this on poultry, game or lamb before cooking.

3
CARIBBEAN

NOTED CHILLIES

Scotch Bonnets (pictured opposite), Caribbean Red Habanero,
Trinidad Moruga Scorpion, Wiri Wiri, Bird peppers.

CHILLI FACTS & FICTION

In Trinidad, chilli pepper leaf tea is served as a remedy for coughs
and sore throats.

As a cure for baldness, hot chilli oil is applied topically to the head.
The resulting tingling, burning sensation is supposed to stimulate
hair growth.

SIMPLE ORANGE & CUMIN MARINADE *(opposite)*

Simple and tasty, this marinade from Cuba needs to be made with Seville or sour oranges because it is their sharpness that makes the marinade. If you can't get hold of any (it can be difficult out of season), use a combination of half orange juice and half lime juice.

zest of 1 orange	2 tsp ground cumin
juice of 4–5 Seville (or sour) oranges	2 tsp chilli powder
1 onion, finely chopped	1 tsp sea salt
8 garlic cloves, finely chopped	½ tsp ground black pepper

Put all the ingredients in a food processor and blend until you have a smooth but quite loose sauce. Store in an airtight jar in the fridge until you are ready to use it.

Hot tip: Use this as a marinade for pork, especially shoulder, before roasting.

SERIOUSLY HOT CHILLI & CITRUS MARINADE

Every couple of days in our house, we get the uncontrollable urge to eat something really fiery, and to be honest this is about as hot as it gets. It can be used as a simple marinade.

4 Scotch Bonnet chillies, deseeded and cut into fine strips	zest and juice of 2 lemons
2 banana shallots, finely sliced	2 tbsp muscovado/molasses sugar
2-cm/¾-inch piece fresh ginger, peeled and cut into fine strips	2 tbsp cider vinegar
5–6 garlic cloves, crushed	1 tsp thyme leaves
1 tsp salt	1 tsp red peppercorns, ground
	½ tsp ground allspice

Put the chillies, shallots, ginger and garlic in a bowl. Sprinkle with the salt and squeeze over the lemon juice. Stir the mixture thoroughly, then set aside for 15 minutes. Add the sugar to the vinegar and stir to break it up. Add the sugar mixture to the chilli mixture followed by the remaining ingredients, and stir together thoroughly. Cover and refrigerate for 1–2 hours to allow the flavours to mingle.

Hot tip: Use this as a brilliant marinade for pork or firm white fish. The sugars in the marinade caramelize deliciously if cooked under a hot grill/broiler or on the barbecue. But beware: this is frighteningly HOT, so use with caution.

MOTHER-IN-LAW SAUCE

1 large carrot

1 onion

½–1 small green karali/bitter melon (or unripe, green mango), deseeded

4 Trinidad Congo (or Scotch Bonnet) hot chillies, deseeded

4 garlic cloves

8 chadon beni leaves (or a small handful of coriander/cilantro)

juice of 2 limes

1 tsp sea salt

cider vinegar, as needed (optional)

There can be few condiments or sauces named in a less exotic or more provocative manner than this piece of sheer genius from Trinidad. It is a kind of salsa–ridiculously hot salad combination, although it can be blended down to make a genuine pourable sauce, which I suspect would store for longer. The name comes from this recipe's fiery tongue that is guaranteed to leave an impression on you.

The key to making this dish work well is to make sure that the ingredients are chopped to approximately the same size. Peel and chop the carrot and onion and put in a large bowl. Chop the karali and add to the mixture. The chillies will need to be chopped slightly more finely, and it is advisable to wear gloves to do this as they are extremely hot! Add these to the bowl, then chop the garlic to about the same size as the chillies. Mix thoroughly in the bowl.

Finely chop the chadon beni leaves and add to the bowl with the lime juice and salt. Mix thoroughly and put in the fridge for a few hours before serving, stirring occasionally.

If you wish to blend this down to a sauce, I would suggest adding a small amount of cider vinegar to loosen the mixture as it is blended. This will also lower its natural pH level giving it a slightly increased storage life in the fridge. As a salsa, I would recommend using this on the day it is made.

Hot tip: Use this as an accompaniment to any barbecued meat or fish, or even as a fiery burger relish.

DAN'S CARIBBEAN CLASSIC

Sometimes all you want is a simple, perfect chilli sauce – and this sauce is just that. Based on a classic Trinidadian recipe, it calls for Scotch Bonnet chillies, which are essential, but if possible, use the Antillais Caribbean strain for their mouthwatering aroma, fruitiness and balance of flavour, heat and acidity.

1 tbsp cider vinegar

½ tsp mustard seeds

50 g/1¾ oz. Scotch Bonnet chillies (stalks removed), halved

1 tsp lemon juice

1 garlic clove, crushed

½ tsp salt

1 tsp lime juice

Gently warm the vinegar in a small saucepan over medium heat and add the mustard seeds. Cover and set aside for at least 1 hour to allow the seeds to soften a little. Add the chillies, 1 tablespoon water, the lemon juice, garlic and salt to the pan, and return to the heat. Heat to a gentle simmer and cook until the chillies have softened a little. Use a stick blender (or transfer to a blender) to process the ingredients to a smooth sauce consistency. (You may need to do this in a smaller container to allow the blender blades to be covered and to operate effectively.)

Return to the heat and add the lime juice. Bring back to a gentle simmer and cook for 2 minutes, stirring regularly. If the sauce seems a little thick, add a few tablespoons more water. Blend again if required.

Pour into a sterilized bottle and seal tightly. Allow to cool, then store in the fridge until you are ready to use it. The flavours will mingle and improve over the next few weeks. I have kept an open bottle of this sauce in my fridge for several months with no noticeable change in appearance or taste, so you can double or treble these ingredients and make up a larger batch.

Hot tip: Use this with anything and everything that needs a little hit.

ANTILLAIS CAPER & SCOTCH BONNET SAUCE

This sauce takes the classic flavour of capers and gives it a huge kick of fiery, fruity Scotch Bonnet – perfect with the lime juice and fresh herbs.

1 banana shallot (or other large shallot), roughly chopped

1 garlic clove, roughly chopped

a small handful of coriander/cilantro, chopped

a few flat-leaf parsley and/or tarragon leaves, chopped

juice of 1½–2 limes

2 tbsp good-quality olive oil

1 tbsp capers, rinsed and chopped

1 tbsp Cabernet Sauvignon vinegar

1–2 Antillais Caribbean Scotch Bonnet chillies, deseeded

sea salt and black pepper

Put all the ingredients in a blender or food processor and pulse until you have a smooth and fragrant sauce. Add 1–2 tablespoons water to loosen the sauce if it is a little thick. Season with salt and pepper, to taste. Set aside for about 10–15 minutes to allow the flavours to combine. Enjoy!

Hot tip: Use this to serve with fresh grilled/broiled or barbecued fish – mackerel would be perfect.

ANTILLAIS FISH MARINADE

The French Antilles are in many ways the gem of the Caribbean when it comes to cuisine. This marinade uses the Antillais Caribbean Scotch Bonnet, which to my mind is simply the best Scotch Bonnet out there – it also grows rather well on a warm windowsill in the UK!

4½ tbsp lime juice

1 tsp sea salt

3 thyme sprigs, leaves stripped and chopped

1 tsp mixed peppercorns, ground

3 garlic cloves, chopped

1–2 Antillais Caribbean Scotch Bonnet (or other Scotch Bonnet) chillies, deseeded

Put all the ingredients in a food processor or blender and process until you have a smooth paste. Scrape into a large resealable food bag and refrigerate until you are ready to use it.

Hot tip: This is a simple marinade designed for fish – and being Caribbean it is wonderfully HOT! Use this to coat red snapper, but any firm-fleshed fish would do – try monkfish. To use, add the fish to the bag, reseal it and give the bag a really good shake. Marinate for about 20 minutes.

CRAB, LIME & SCOTCH BONNET SAUCE

I love this French Caribbean sauce. It takes a few of my favourite flavours and combines them to make a delicious and slightly unusual sauce. Crab seems to have been created to go with hot chillies.

1 tbsp groundnut oil

1 onion, finely chopped

2 garlic cloves, finely chopped

1 Scotch Bonnet chilli, deseeded and finely chopped

1 carrot, finely chopped

50 ml/scant ¼ cup lime juice (juice of 1½–2 limes)

about 2 tbsp coconut milk

175-g/6-oz. can white crab meat, drained (120 g/4¼ oz. drained weight)

1 tsp paprika

1 tsp thyme leaves

1 tsp rosemary leaves, finely chopped

a small handful of chives

sea salt and black pepper

Heat the oil in a medium saucepan over medium heat and fry the onion for 5 minutes, or until it begins to colour and soften (do not let it burn). Add the garlic and chilli and fry for another 1–2 minutes, stirring to stop the ingredients sticking to the pan.

Add the carrot, lime juice and 2 tablespoons coconut milk. Stir to combine and bring to a gentle simmer. Add hot water or more coconut milk if the sauce is too dry. Stir in the crab meat, then simmer gently until the carrots are cooked. Stir in the paprika, thyme and rosemary, then remove from the heat. Using a blender or stick blender, blitz the mixture to an even but still slightly coarse-textured sauce. Snip the chives into the sauce and stir through. Season to taste with salt and pepper.

This sauce is great served from the pan on warm foods or transferred to an airtight container and placed in the fridge to chill to room temperature to be used as a salad dressing. This will keep for several days, sealed, in the fridge.

Hot tip: Use this in a white sauce to pep up a fish pie or with a potato salad. Also perfect for dressing fresh fish fillets that have been lightly grilled/broiled and is remarkably good with a salad, especially egg and avocado.

CARIBBEAN BLACK BEAN & MANGO SALSA

This is a fantastic alternative to the kind of 'regular' salsas that we always see served with nachos. This recipe is somewhere around medium heat and is perfect for a family barbecue.

400-g/14-oz. can black beans, rinsed and drained

1 small mango, finely chopped

1 small red onion, chopped

1 small hot fresh chilli, deseeded and very finely chopped

1 small green sweet/bell pepper, deseeded and chopped

2 plum tomatoes, deseeded and chopped

juice of 1 small lime

1 tbsp cider vinegar

½ tsp garlic salt

½ tsp Cajun spice blend

½ tsp cayenne pepper

a small handful of coriander/cilantro, chopped

Put the beans in a medium bowl with the mango, onion, chilli, green pepper, tomatoes, lime juice and vinegar. Turn them gently together to avoid breaking up the individual pieces of fruit and veg.

Season with the garlic salt, Cajun spice blend and cayenne pepper and carefully mix through, making sure that everything is evenly covered. Just before serving, add the coriander and stir gently to combine.

Hot tip: Use this as a great dip for nachos or as a summer-barbecue salsa. If you want to up the heat a little, I would recommend using a finely diced fiery Scotch Bonnet or Habanero chilli and maybe a dry jerk seasoning in place of the Cajun spice.

HOT CHILLI COCONUT DIP

This is a hot and exotic dip that brings together creamy coconut, fruity mango and devilishly hot chillies in an original and surprising dip. Adding the hot oil to the fresh ingredients just takes the edge off their raw flavours without cooking them. Ensure that all the ingredients are well mixed together before refrigerating so that every mouthful contains sweet, sour, herby and hot flavours.

1 tbsp vegetable oil

3 Habanero chillies, (ideally Trinidad Congo, Antillais Caribbean, Orange Habanero), deseeded and finely chopped

2 large spring onions/scallions, thinly sliced

2 garlic cloves, crushed

½ tsp thyme leaves

1 tsp salt

250 ml/1 cup coconut milk

50 g/1¾ oz. ripe avocado, mashed

50 g/1¾ oz. mango, cut into 1-cm/½-inch dice

1 tbsp cider vinegar

zest and juice of 1 lime

coriander/cilantro and ground black pepper, to garnish (optional)

Heat the oil in a small saucepan over medium heat until hot.

Put the chillies, onions, garlic, thyme and salt in a small heatproof bowl and pour the hot oil over. Stir as the oil cools a little, then pour off the excess oil.

Clean the pan and pour in the coconut milk, then add the avocado, mango and vinegar. Bring to the boil, stirring frequently. As the first bubbles appear, remove the pan from the heat and pour over the chilli mixture from the bowl. Stir well, then allow to cool a little and add the lime zest and juice. Refrigerate until required. To serve, add chopped coriander and black pepper, if you like.

Hot tip: Use this as a dip for barbecued chicken or veggie kebabs/kabobs.

PRIME MINISTER ERROL BARROW'S HOT CHILLI SAUCE

Errol Barrow was Prime Minister of Barbados, not once but twice. Among his many feats, including being a World War II fighter pilot and a successful barrister, he also produced a cookbook, which was published in 1988 a year after he died. This was his favourite recipe for hot sauce.

12 large Scotch Bonnet chillies, deseeded and chopped

2 onions, roughly chopped

5 small garlic cloves, chopped

2 tbsp English mustard

2 tbsp white wine vinegar

2 tbsp vegetable oil

2 large carrots, finely chopped

sea salt and black pepper

Put the chillies in a saucepan over medium heat and add the onions, garlic, mustard, vinegar, oil and carrots. Measure out 400 ml/1¾ cups water. Add 200 ml/¾ cup water and bring to the boil, stirring frequently. Allow to boil for 15–20 minutes, adding more water if the contents begin to dry out.

Blend all the ingredients using a stick blender or mini food processor to make a smooth purée. Return to the pan and season to taste with the salt and pepper. Adjust the consistency by adding more water if required. Return to the boil and immediately pour into sterilized jars, then seal. Allow to cool and store in the fridge.

Hot tip: Use this as a table condiment for any meat, fish or vegetable dish. This is a classic Bajan hot sauce. It contains no sugar, but you may wish to add 1 tablespoon with the water to slightly sweeten the finished sauce.

RUM, LIME & GINGER MARINADE

Mango, chilli, rum, coconut milk and lime – sounds simple but tastes exotic and fiery. Quite possibly these ingredients make the perfect cocktail as well as the basis for a Caribbean marinade!

½ mango, peeled, pitted and chopped

1 tbsp dark rum

1 Scotch Bonnet chilli, deseeded

2 garlic cloves, crushed

2.5-cm/1-inch piece fresh ginger, peeled and chopped

½ tsp ground coriander

a pinch of ground cumin

a pinch of sea salt

50 ml/scant ¼ cup coconut milk

juice of 1 lime

a small bunch of coriander/cilantro, finely chopped

Put the mango, rum, chilli, garlic and ginger in a small food processor and blend to a smooth paste.

Transfer to a small pan and heat gently over medium heat, then add the remaining spices, salt and coconut milk. Bring to a gentle simmer and add the lime juice. Cook for 5 minutes and add the coriander. Remove from the heat, pour into a sterilized container and seal tightly. Let cool before using.

Hot tip: Use this as a marinade for vegetables or fish.

ADOBO MOJADO

An 'adobo' was the original Spanish means of preserving meat. Today, it is a popular marinade for meat and fish in Spanish-speaking Central American and Caribbean countries.

6–8 garlic cloves, crushed

2 tbsp paprika (or 1 tbsp each paprika and Ancho chilli powder)

1 tbsp salt

1 tbsp dried oregano

1 green Jalapeño chilli, deseeded and chopped

125 ml/½ cup vegetable oil

50 ml/scant ¼ cup cider vinegar

2 tbsp lime or orange juice, or a mixture of both

1 tsp brown sugar

½ tsp ground cumin

Put all the ingredients in a food processor and blend to a smooth paste. Store in a sealed jar in the fridge until you are ready to use. I would keep this paste for a week before using it to allow the flavours to mingle, merge and improve.

Hot tip: Use this to marinate any meat, fish or seafood dish before cooking.

4
MEDITERRANEAN

NOTED CHILLIES

Piment D'Espelette, Pimentón (paprika – pictured opposite, right),
Peperoncini, Bulgarian Carrot (pictured opposite, left),
Hungarian Hot Wax.

CHILLI FACTS & FICTION

Calabria in Italy is home to the world's only chilli pepper museum:
the Museo del Peperoncino.

HOT PEPPER HONEY

Whether it's made with peppercorns or chillies (see right), hot honey makes the perfect spicy accompaniment for any dish. Serve this briny, peppery honey directly drizzled over cheese or just whisked into a vinaigrette for an accompanying salad.

1 string of brined green peppercorns (if you can't buy strings of peppercorns, use 2 tbsp instead)
1 cup/280 g organic wildflower runny honey

sterilized glass jar with an airtight lid

Place the peppercorns in a sterilized glass jar with a tightly-fitting lid. Pour in the honey and screw on the lid. Leave to infuse for 1 week before using. The longer you leave the honey, the more intense the taste.

HOT CHILLI HONEY

This hot chilli honey will become your new best friend! Drizzle it over cheese, over pizza, over a peanut butter bagel, add to a stir-fry, mix it into a salsa for some added pep or use it as a glaze on chicken wings – the uses really are endless!

2–3 tbsp dried chilli/hot red pepper flakes, crushed dried chillies or 2–3 fresh sliced hot chillies
1 cup/280 g organic wildflower runny honey

sterilized glass jar with an airtight lid

Place the chillies in a sterilized glass jar with a tightly-fitting lid. Pour in the honey and screw on the lid. Leave to infuse for 1 week before using. The longer you leave the honey, the more intense the taste.

ROUILLE

This delicious French chilli pick-me-up is a recipe that I seem to remember knowing forever. I have no idea when or where I tried it first, but I travelled regularly in the South of France in the past and particularly during the late autumn. I pretty quickly became a fan of bouillabaisse (the classic fish soup). Rouille is often employed to give this classic a little kick. I loved the warming chilli hit, especially when eaten outside in the last few days of autumn sunshine.

1 slice of stale white bread, crusts removed

1 red sweet/bell pepper, roasted, peeled and roughly chopped

2 plump garlic cloves, roughly chopped

a good glug of fine olive oil

2 medium-heat red chillies, deseeded and chopped

sea salt and black pepper

Soak the bread in a little water to soften it for a few minutes. Squeeze out the excess water and combine the bread with the red pepper and the remaining ingredients.

Using a blender or food processor, blend the mixture until you have a smooth paste. Season with salt and pepper to taste. Transfer to a serving bowl and set aside until you are ready to use it.

Hot tip: Use this added to a bowl of simple fish soup (a spoonful or two of Rouille), or even Spanish garlic soup after serving.

ROSEMARY & CHILLI-INFUSED VINEGAR

I love to make this with sherry vinegar and use it to deglaze roasted dishes. The rosemary flavouring works fantastically well with roast lamb and, when mixed with the roasting juices, provides a great base for a rich gravy or reduced sauce.

2 dried rosemary sprigs (see method for drying)

6 small dried red chillies, such as tiny, hot Zimbabwe Bird chillies

500 ml/2 cups good-quality wine vinegar or sherry vinegar

2 garlic cloves, unpeeled, pierced several times using a cocktail stick/ toothpick or sharp knife

If you need to dry your rosemary and chillies, the simplest way to do this is to put them on a baking sheet in an oven preheated to 70°C (150°F) Gas ¼. Leave the door slightly ajar to allow the moisture to evaporate from the fruit and herbs. The rosemary and chillies should still maintain a little flexibility after drying. If they are completely desiccated they will fall to pieces in the vinegar. Drying the flavourings means that the only moisture left in them will be the flavour-rich oils that we want to transfer into the vinegar.

Sterilize 2 × 250 ml/1 cup bottles with tight seals. In a large saucepan, heat the vinegar over medium heat until it just begins to boil, then add the chillies and garlic. Reduce the heat and gently simmer for 5 minutes.

Push one rosemary sprig into each bottle. Divide the chillies and garlic evenly between the bottles and immediately pour the hot vinegar into the bottles leaving at least a 2-cm/¾-inch air gap at the top. Seal tightly and shake. Allow to cool naturally and put in a cool, dark place to infuse for at least 2 weeks or preferably up to 2 months. Turn the bottles regularly to aid infusion.

Hot tip: Use this to make salad dressings, in tomato sauces, to deglaze roasting dishes or to make quick vegetable pickles.

SUPER-SPEEDY PATATAS BRAVAS SAUCE

Here is a great way to get all those delicious smoky, tomatoey Spanish flavours on the table in no time. It's ideal as a dip or as a speedy treat. Add some 1-cm/½-inch cubes of chorizo when you are frying the onions and you'll have an impromptu, but delicious, pasta sauce.

2 tbsp olive oil

1 onion, finely chopped

2 garlic cloves, crushed

225 g/8 oz. passata (Italian sieved tomatoes)

1 tsp paprika

½ tsp spicy smoked paprika (Pimentón Piccante)

1 tbsp red wine vinegar

a good pinch of sea salt

a pinch of sugar

1 tsp dried oregano

chopped flat-leaf parsley

Heat the oil in a medium saucepan over medium heat. Add the onion and fry for 2–3 minutes. Add the garlic and fry for a further 1 minute.

Pour in the passata. Add the paprikas, vinegar, salt, sugar and oregano. Stir thoroughly, then turn up the heat and bring the mixture to the boil. Reduce the heat and simmer for a further 5 minutes, stirring regularly. Add the parsley, mix well and serve.

Hot tip: Use this as a dip for fried potatoes or wedges – use as a kind of Spanish ketchup.

SALSA VERDE PICCANTE

It pains me to say it but I have never been a 'green' fan. Combining the deliciousness of parsley, basil and mint with capers and with lemon, garlic and anchovy changes everything for me.

a handful of flat-leaf parsley, chopped

a small handful of basil, torn

a few mint leaves, chopped

2–3 tbsp capers

zest of 1 lemon

1 small hot green chilli, deseeded and finely chopped

6 anchovy fillets, drained, rinsed, dried and chopped

1 garlic clove, crushed

1 hot green chilli, deseeded and very finely chopped

1 tbsp extra virgin olive oil, or as needed

sea salt and black pepper

Put all the ingredients into a large mortar and mash to a rough paste using a pestle. Alternatively, put all the ingredients into a food processor and pulse briefly for a few seconds. Loosen with extra olive oil as required and season with a little salt and pepper.

This salsa is wonderfully robust so don't be afraid to experiment with the herbs used. If you have a glut of one herb, throw it in! My own favourite variations use freshly picked wild garlic leaves or garden-grown French tarragon.

Hot tip: Use this to serve with fish or to stuff a fish you are roasting; with smoked salmon as a bold filling for canapés.

PERFECT SPANISH SEASONING PASTE

Early mornings are an abiding memory of all my trips to Spain – taking photographs as the sun rose, and now loving being at the market with the locals getting everything fresh from the fields. This recipe is a distillation of all those fresh ingredients, spices and colours. The pure essence of Spain in tastes and smells!

a few saffron threads

50 ml/scant ¼ cup warmed fish stock or water

1 tbsp olive oil

4 shallots, finely chopped

4 garlic cloves, finely chopped

1 tbsp sherry vinegar

2 tbsp tomato purée/ paste

1 tsp vegetable bouillon powder

1 tsp Pimentón Dulce

½ tsp Pimentón Piccante

½ tsp dried chilli/hot red pepper flakes

a small handful of flat-leaf parsley, finely chopped

sea salt and black pepper

Put the saffron in a small bowl and add the stock. Allow to infuse/steep for 20–30 minutes. Meanwhile, heat a medium frying pan/skillet over a medium-low heat, add the oil and shallots and cook for 5 minutes, or until they begin to soften. Add the garlic and cook, stirring frequently, until the onions are soft. Add the vinegar, tomato purée, bouillon powder, both types of paprika and the chilli flakes. Mix well and add the saffron-infused stock. Cook over low heat for 3 minutes, stirring frequently.

Pour the mixture into a blender or mini food processor and pulse to a smooth paste. Season with salt and pepper, then add the parsley. Blend briefly to mix. The paste should be thick, glossy and smooth. If it is too thick, add a little boiled water or warmed stock, and blend again. If the paste is a little loose, return it to the pan and gently cook, stirring constantly, until the mixture reduces. The paste will thicken a little when it cools. Pack immediately into a sterilized jar and cool then refrigerate.

Hot tip: Use this to flavour Bomba or Arborio rice dishes; as a base for a chorizo and seafood stew; in a tasty, quick monkfish paella.

MARINADE FOR PINCHITOS MORUNOS

Pinchitos Morunos is a classic Andalusian tapas dish. The name actually translates literally to 'Moorish Spikes'. Pork, lamb or chicken is marinated in this spicy sauce before being skewered and cooked, traditionally on a wood-fired barbecue. Tapas has to be the most exciting way to get children to try new foods that in any other circumstance they would firmly believe they didn't like. On their first trip to Spain, both my older boys discovered that they actually loved squid, which they would never have tried at home.

a few saffron threads

1 tsp sweet smoked paprika (Pimentón Dulce)

½ tsp sea salt

½ tsp coriander seeds

½ tsp ground cumin

½ tsp fennel seeds

1 tsp dried oregano

1 bay leaf, central stalk discarded, finely chopped

2 garlic cloves, finely chopped

2 tsp sherry vinegar

2 tsp olive oil

Put the saffron in a small jar and add 2 tablespoons hot water. Allow to infuse/steep for 20 minutes.

Put the paprika, salt, coriander, cumin, fennel, oregano and bay in a bowl and mix together. Add the garlic, vinegar, oil and the saffron liquid. Stir thoroughly. Transfer to a sterilized glass jar and seal tightly. This will keep in the fridge for several weeks.

Hot tip: Use this to marinate pork, lamb or chicken.

SOFRITO

In many ways Sofrito is the basis of Spanish cooking, but it exists in a variety of forms throughout the Mediterranean, Caribbean and Central America. A classic Spanish Sofrito would have no added chilli beyond the paprika, although the fruity Piquillo chilli is not out of place, adding a delicious zip to the sauce. The option of including some Habanero chilli adds a little punch to the classic recipe.

4 tbsp good-quality olive oil (the choice of oil has a great effect on the final flavour so use the best oil you can, with a flavour you like)

1 large onion, finely chopped

2 garlic cloves, finely chopped

1 large red sweet/bell pepper, deseeded and finely chopped

3 Piquillo chillies, finely chopped

½ Habanero chilli, deseeded and finely chopped (optional)

4 large ripe plum tomatoes, peeled, deseeded and chopped

1 fresh bay leaf

1 thyme sprig

½ tsp paprika

sea salt and black pepper

Heat a heavy-based saucepan over medium heat and add the oil. Add the onion and fry, stirring regularly, until it turns golden brown and caramelized. It is very important not to allow the onion to burn or stick to the pan, but it is equally important to ensure the heat is high enough to cook it evenly.

Add the garlic, red pepper and chillies and fry for 3–4 minutes until they soften without over-browning. Add the tomatoes, bay leaf and thyme and cook for a further 15 minutes, stirring frequently. Stir in the paprika and cook for 5 minutes. Remove from the heat and season well with salt and pepper to taste. Remove the bay leaf and the thyme sprig.

Hot tip: Use this as the perfect sauce for homemade pizza. It can also be used as a delicious substitute for regular tomato purée/paste in any dish. See also the Fra Diavolo sauce opposite.

FRA DIAVOLO SAUCE

This sauce can be added to some fresh tomatoes to make a fantastic Italian 'all'arrabiata' sauce for pasta. Fra Diavolo literally translates as 'Brother Devil'.

2 tbsp olive oil

3 shallots, finely chopped

4–5 garlic cloves, crushed

2 Peperone red sweet/bell peppers (or Romano), finely chopped

100 g/3½ oz. mixed red chillies, such as Ciliega, Naso di Cane and Amando or Cherry Bomb, Red Jalapeño and Ring of Fire cayenne, finely chopped

3 tbsp red wine vinegar

2 tbsp tomato purée/paste (or Sofrito – see opposite)

1 tsp dried oregano

1 tsp sea salt, or to taste

black pepper

Heat the oil in a heavy-based saucepan over medium-low heat. Add the shallots and fry gently for 5 minutes, or until they soften. Add the garlic, red peppers and chillies and continue to gently fry for 10 minutes.

Add the vinegar, tomato purée and oregano, then stir well and allow to gently simmer for another 20 minutes, adding a little water if the consistency becomes too dry. Season with salt and pepper to taste. The sauce can be blended into a smoother consistency, if you like, or stored in a sterilized jar as a chunky paste.

Hot tip: Use this as the basis for a great seafood sauce served with fresh pasta.

MALLORCAN ROMESCU SAUCE *(opposite)*

During a spring break to Mallorca we spent most of the week cooking all our food in a huge traditional wood-fired oven. It took many hours and piles of wood, but the flavour of the food was superb. I was served this sauce in a bar in Pollensa alongside grilled fish. You can use Pimentón Piccante if you prefer a smoky, hotter flavour.

5 large ripe vine-ripened tomatoes

1 large garlic bulb

100 g/3½ oz. toasted almonds, finely chopped

1 tsp dried chilli/hot red pepper flakes

125 ml/½ cup good-quality extra virgin olive oil

1 tbsp sweet paprika, or to taste

1–2 tbsp sherry vinegar, preferably Jerez sherry vinegar

½ tsp sea salt, or to taste

Wrap each tomato and the bulb of garlic individually in foil. Roast in a hot wood-fired oven (or in a regular oven preheated to 200°C (400°F) Gas 6, or directly on the embers of your barbecue). Peel the tomatoes and put in a large mortar. Squeeze the roasted garlic cloves out of their skins into the mortar. Start to work these together using a pestle.

Add the almonds, chilli, oil and paprika. Work together to form a fairly coarse but well mixed paste. Add the vinegar and salt according to taste. You can also add more paprika, if you like.

Hot tip: Use this with fish or meat or as a dip for the traditional Mallorcan nibble of spring onions/scallions lightly charred over the fire.

SHERRY VINEGAR & SMOKED PAPRIKA MARINADE

Here is a lovely southern Spanish marinade with Moorish overtones of cumin and lemon. We first made this recipe in the hills outside Ronda, Andalusia. We scored a leg of lamb, marinated it for several hours in this blend and then roasted it in a hot oven, with potatoes roasted in the fat from the meat.

2 tbsp sherry vinegar

3 tbsp olive oil

2 garlic cloves, crushed

1 tsp cumin seeds

2 tsp coarse sea salt

1 tsp hot smoked paprika (Pimentón Piccante)

1 tsp sweet smoked paprika (Pimentón Dulce)

1 dried bay leaf, central stalk discarded, finely chopped

1 tsp rosemary leaves, finely chopped

zest and juice from ½ lemon

Pour the vinegar and oil into a bowl. Add the garlic and whisk together. Put the cumin seeds and salt in a mortar and use a pestle to crush them lightly together.

Tip the cumin-seed mixture into the bowl with the garlic, and add the hot and sweet paprikas, the herbs, and lemon zest and juice. Mix thoroughly together.

Hot tip: Use this as a marinade for lamb and chicken before roasting, or even with mackerel.

JORDANIAN BAHARAT BLEND *(opposite, left)*

When I discovered the heady aromas of freshly ground Baharat (which, incidentally, is simply Arabic for 'spice'), it immediately took me back to a family trip to the Middle East and the wonderfully fragrant aubergine/eggplant and lentil stews I had eaten.

1 tbsp red peppercorns	½ tbsp cardamom pods
1 tbsp mixed peppercorns (black, green and white)	½ tbsp grated nutmeg
1½ tbsp coriander seeds	4 tbsp sweet paprika
1½ tbsp cumin seeds	½ tsp ground cinnamon
½ tbsp allspice berries	1 tsp dried chilli/hot red pepper flakes
2 tsp cloves	

Put the peppercorns in a heavy-based saucepan over medium heat and add the coriander seeds, cumin seeds, allspice berries, cloves and cardamom pods. Lightly toast the seeds, tossing the pan regularly. Remove from the heat and allow to cool. Remove the cardamom seeds from the toasted pods and discard the empty pods.

Put all the ingredients in a mortar, and combine using a pestle until you have a fairly fine and even grind. (Alternatively, use a food processor or grinder.) The blend will smell fantastic. I use it as an integral part of my Moroccan Tagine Paste (see page 24). Transfer to an airtight container and store in a cool, dark place. It will happily keep for several months if stored in this way.

Hot tip: Use this for cooking lentils, aubergine/eggplant, lamb, chicken and venison.

ZA'ATAR SPICE BLEND
(opposite, middle)

This blend is a tasty variation on the za'atar theme. It's a herb and sesame combination that works well as a topping for sweet or savoury dishes, and it's great as an alternative to dukkah.

2 tsp sesame seeds	1 tsp sea salt
2 tsp dried oregano	1½ tsp ground cumin
2 tsp ground sumac	
3 tsp thyme leaves, finely chopped (use wild thyme, if you can get it)	

Put the sesame seeds in a small saucepan over medium heat and toast for 2 minutes, or until they begin to brown. Remove from the heat and put half the seeds in a blender with the other ingredients and pulse for 10–20 seconds. Tip into a bowl and stir in the remaining sesame seeds. Store in an airtight jar in the fridge for up to 1 week.

Hot tip: Use this to sprinkle on hummus, cooked meat or vegetables. Or to finish a salad, with fresh pitta bread to dip in olive oil and then to coat with the spice mix.

MUHAMMARA *(below, right)*

4 red sweet/bell peppers

1 tsp cumin seeds

100 g/⅔ cup walnuts

a good handful of fresh breadcrumbs

2–3 garlic cloves

1–2 tbsp lemon juice

2 tsp pomegranate molasses

1 tbsp dried chilli/hot red pepper flakes

125 ml/½ cup extra virgin olive oil

sea salt and black pepper

Although a Syrian speciality, Muhammara is now popular throughout the Eastern Mediterranean. This spicy red pepper dip is served in much the same way as hummus. Use it to dip pitta bread or carrot sticks into, or serve it as a sauce for grilled meat and fish.

Spear the red peppers onto a long fork or metal skewer and carefully fire-roast them over a naked flame, or put under a hot grill/broiler until the skins start to blacken and blister. Put the peppers in a plastic food bag and tie the top. Leave for 10 minutes, or until the skins to start to peel away from the flesh.

Meanwhile, put the cumin seeds in heavy-based saucepan over medium heat and lightly toast, tossing the pan frequently. Put them in a mortar and grind using the pestle. Toast the walnuts in the same way, then roughly chop them.

Remove the roasted peppers from the bag and peel, deseed and roughly chop the flesh. Put the peppers, ground cumin and chopped walnuts in a food processor and add the breadcrumbs, garlic, lemon juice, molasses, chilli flakes and oil. Blend to a smooth paste and season to taste with salt and pepper. Put in an airtight container and refrigerate until you are ready to use it. The flavours will continue to improve as they 'mingle' if stored for a few days. It is always preferable to allow Muhammara to come to room temperature before serving.

Hot tip: Use this as a tasty alternative to hummus.

5
USA

NOTED CHILLIES

Serrano, Jalapeño, Chiltepin, Datil, Anaheim (pictured opposite, right),
Santa Fe (pictured opposite, left), Cubanelle, Cascabel, Cayenne.

CHILLI FACTS & FICTION

In the Deep South, legend holds that in order to grow hot peppers you
need to be angry when you plant them – the hottest peppers are by
default thought to be grown by lunatics!

CREOLE RÉMOULADE *(below, left)*

Rémoulade takes a classic mayonnaise and adds capers, shallots, tarragon, parsley and, of course, hot sauce. Adding finely chopped fresh chillies works excellently in this recipe.

2 large egg yolks

1 tbsp Dijon mustard

250 ml/1 cup olive oil

1 tsp Tabasco or other Louisiana-style hot sauce

¼ tsp sea salt

a good pinch of freshly ground white pepper

1 tbsp lemon juice

1 shallot, finely chopped

2 tsp capers, finely chopped

a very small bunch of tarragon

a few flat-leaf parsley leaves

½ chilli, preferably Habanero, finely chopped (optional)

Put the egg yolks in a large mixing bowl and add the mustard. Whisk gently with a balloon whisk to break up the eggs and mix evenly. This is where it gets useful to have another pair of hands: briskly and evenly whisk the egg mixture while slowly adding the oil into the edge of the mixture in a thin ribbon – the slower this is added at the early stages the less likely the mayonnaise is to separate.

Once all the oil is blended, keep whisking and add the Tabasco, salt, pepper and lemon juice. Stir in the shallot, capers, tarragon, parsley and chilli (if using).

Hot tip: Use this to serve with fish and chips, or boiled new potatoes.

LOUISIANA SPICY SAUCE

(opposite, right)

This sauce is super-easy to make and cook with. My preferred way to use it has to be this Creole fish bake: pour the sauce over 2 firm-fleshed fish fillets in the morning, cover with foil and leave in the fridge; in the evening, roast the fish at 180°C (350°F) Gas 4 for 20–30 minutes or until it begins to flake with a fork.

15 g/1 tbsp butter

1 onion, finely chopped

1 garlic clove, crushed

2 red sweet/bell peppers, deseeded and finely chopped

4 medium-heat chillies, deseeded and finely chopped

1 tbsp red wine vinegar

400-g/14-oz. can chopped tomatoes

1 tsp sea salt

1 bay leaf

2 tsp dried thyme

½ tsp ground black pepper

½ tsp cayenne pepper

¼ tsp ground cinnamon

Heat the butter in a heavy-based frying pan/skillet over medium heat and gently fry the onion for 2 minutes. Add the garlic and fry for a further 1 minute.

Add the red peppers and the chillies and fry for about 3–4 minutes. Add the remaining ingredients, bring gently to the bowl, then reduce the heat and simmer for 45 minutes. Remove the bay leaf and allow to cool.

Hot tip: Use this as a marinade or cook-in-sauce for any meat or fish.

CAJUN BLACKENING SPICE

All you need to do to make this spice blend is add the ingredients to a jar and shake.

2 tbsp dried thyme

1 tbsp soft brown sugar

1 tbsp sweet paprika

2 tsp dried onion powder

2 tsp ground black pepper

1½ tsp sea salt

1 tsp garlic powder

1 tsp cayenne pepper

1 tsp dried oregano

¾ tsp ground cumin

½ tsp grated nutmeg

½ tsp ground allspice

2 bay leaves, central stalk discarded, finely chopped

Put all the ingredients in a sealable jar. Close the lid and shake until everything is evenly mixed. Store in a cool dark place until needed.

Hot tip: Use this mixed with a little flour as a coating for chicken or fish before frying or barbecuing.

SPICY BROWN ROUX FOR GUMBO *(opposite, left)*

Cajun food lends itself to spicy, hearty one-pot dishes that make the most of the many vegetables and fruit that grow in the fertile soil in Louisiana. It is also home to the beer method of measuring cooking times: for example, a 2-beer recipe needs to be cooked for the amount of time it takes to drink 2 beers. A good brown roux is definitely a 4-beer recipe – you have been warned!

275 g/2 sticks plus 3 tbsp salted butter

2 onions, finely chopped

4–5 garlic cloves, finely chopped

1 green sweet/bell pepper, deseeded and finely chopped

1 celery stick, finely chopped

4 medium-heat chillies, such as a mix of Jalapeño, Serrano, Cayenne and De Arbol, finely chopped

250 g/2 cups plain/all-purpose flour

Louisiana hot sauce, to taste

sea salt and black pepper

Melt 25 g/2 tablespoons of the butter in a heavy-based saucepan over medium-low heat. Add the onions and fry very gently for 3 minutes, then add the garlic, green pepper and celery. Continue to fry gently until all the ingredients soften. Stir in the chillies, then fry for another 5 minutes over low heat. Transfer to a bowl and set aside.

Wipe out the pan and add the remaining butter. Reheat over medium heat until the butter melts. Slowly add the flour, a little at a time, stirring constantly. Be very careful to ensure that the roux mixture does not burn or catch on the pan (this would render it useless and you would need to start again). You should notice the flour beginning to brown. Keep stirring and cooking for 15 minutes, or until the roux takes on a rich, almost chocolate-brown colour. This is the perfect colour for making gumbo.

Add the reserved fried ingredients to the pan and stir them through the roux – be patient and try to ensure that everything is evenly mixed. Add seasoning and hot sauce to taste. Remove from the heat and allow to cool. Store in the fridge until required. It is good to make the roux in advance, as storing it will help the flavours to blend together.

Hot tip: Use this to make a major pot of flavourful chicken and smoked-sausage gumbo.

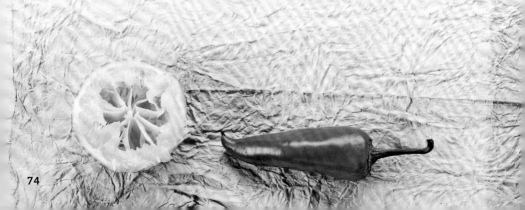

ZESTY CAJUN SEAFOOD SAUCE *(below, right)*

The 'holy trinity' of Cajun cooking (celery, green sweet/bell pepper and onion) is used to create the classic flavour combination for this sauce, designed to smother on fish or seafood before cooking.

4 tbsp tomato purée/ paste

zest and juice of 1 lime

1 onion, finely chopped

½ celery stick, finely chopped

2 Jalapeño or Serrano chillies, finely chopped

½ green sweet/bell pepper, finely chopped

4 pitted green olives, finely chopped

1 tbsp olive oil

1 tsp muscovado/ molasses sugar

a splash of Worcestershire sauce

sea salt and black pepper

Combine all the ingredients in a bowl. Mix well and season with salt and pepper. Store in a tightly sealed jar in the fridge until you are ready to use it.

Hot tip: For an interesting and entirely non-traditional twist, you can try substituting some smoky-flavoured Chipotle chillies that have been gently rehydrated in a little warm cider vinegar instead of using the fresh chillies.

ROAST TOMATO, GARLIC & JALAPEÑO KETCHUP

I first made this recipe with Black Russian tomatoes – a misshapen bowling-ball of a tomato that I love to grow. Unlike normal tomatoes, to make up to the 2 kg/4½ lbs. needed for the recipe we only need 4–5 of the Black Russian tomatoes; however, you do not need to make the sauce from a single variety of tomato and, in fact, using a good mix of varieties will result in a very balanced flavour.

BASE ROAST TOMATO SAUCE

2 kg/4½ lbs. very ripe tomatoes, halved

2–3 fresh bay leaves

2–3 thyme sprigs

2–3 tbsp good-quality olive oil

1 garlic bulb

sea salt and black pepper

triturator (optional)

BASE ROAST TOMATO SAUCE

Preheat the oven to 180°C (350°F) Gas 4. Put the halved tomatoes in a ceramic roasting dish, cut-side up. Pack them quite closely together so that they do not fall over. Push the bay and thyme in among the tomatoes, drizzle with the olive oil and season with salt and pepper.

Using a sharp knife, slice off the top of the garlic bulb, drizzle with olive oil and wrap in foil, creating a flat base so that the bulb will stand upright. Put this in the centre of the dish among the tomatoes. Roast for 45 minutes, or until the tomato skins have begun to char and the flesh has softened. Remove the foil-wrapped garlic and tip the remaining contents of the dish (including all the oil) into a triturator and turn the handle to separate the skin and seeds from the flesh. (Alternatively, rub the mixture through a sieve/strainer using the back of a spoon into a large bowl. Discard the seeds, skins and herbs.

Unwrap the garlic bulb and squeeze the flesh of each clove from its papery shell into the roasted tomato. Stir the roasted garlic flesh into the sauce. Put an airtight covering over the bowl and transfer to the fridge. Leave for several hours to mature – preferably overnight.

KETCHUP

Base Roast Tomato Sauce (see left)

3–4 red Jalapeño chillies, deseeded and very finely chopped, or to taste

100 ml/scant ½ cup cider vinegar, or to taste

100 g/½ cup muscovado/molasses sugar, or to taste

1 tsp celery seeds

1 tsp dried onion powder

1 tbsp sweet paprika

1 tbsp ground black pepper

½ tsp dried oregano

½ tsp ground allspice

½ tsp ground coriander

¼ tsp ground cumin

¼ tsp cayenne pepper

a good pinch of ground mace

a good pinch of ground cinnamon

1 tsp sea salt, or to taste

KETCHUP

Put the Base Roast Tomato Sauce and the remaining ingredients in a large heavy-based saucepan over medium-low heat and gently heat, stirring constantly, until all the sugar has dissolved. Bring to a simmer and continue to cook over low heat for 45 minutes. Taste and season with more salt, sugar or vinegar as required. At this point I often give the mixture a blitz using a stick blender or food processor to ensure the sauce is velvety smooth.

Return to the heat and continue to cook, stirring regularly, until you have achieved the consistency of ketchup you like. Pour into sterilized bottles or jars and seal with an airtight lid. This ketchup should keep for up to a month in the fridge.

Hot tip: You can easily make the ketchup using canned tomatoes, or preferably passata (Italian sieved tomatoes). Be sure to add some roasted garlic, a little olive oil and perhaps some additional herbs at the ketchup-making stage to give you some added flavour. It is also a great idea to make this with other chillies. This recipe is brilliant with fruity Habaneros substituted for the Jalapeños.

TEXAS-STYLE HOT GREEN CHILLI SAUCE
(opposite, top)

Depending on where you live, you may only have come across canned tomatillos in a briny solution, and as such, they bear no relation to the real things at all. They grow well, however, so if you have managed to grow tomatoes, think about planting a few tomatillos alongside them. In Texas they are commonplace and provide the green colour for this sauce – the standard sauce for enchiladas. It's also great with nachos!

500 g/1 lb. 2 oz. tomatillos, roasted under a hot grill/broiler

4 spring onions/scallions, roughly chopped

a small handful of coriander/cilantro, chopped

2–3 garlic cloves, roughly chopped

½ tsp sugar

juice from ½ lime

5–6 Serrano chillies, deseeded

1 tsp vegetable bouillon powder

½ tsp dried mushroom powder

Squeeze the contents of the blackened tomatillos into a food processor or blender. If they are at all tough, discard the skins. Add the remaining ingredients and pulse until all the ingredients are evenly blended.

Pour the mixture into a small saucepan over medium heat and bring gently to a simmer. Cook for about 5–10 minutes until softened, and serve.

Hot tip: Use this as an alternative salsa for nachos, on enchiladas or on grilled/broiled fish.

NEW MEXICAN GREEN CHILLI SAUCE *(opposite, bottom)*

Unlike their neighbours' version in Texas, a New Mex green chilli sauce is very unlikely to contain tomatillos, and the colour comes exclusively from the green chillies used to make the sauce.

2 tbsp vegetable oil

1 onion, finely chopped

2 garlic cloves, finely chopped

1 tbsp flour

½ tsp ground cumin

300 ml/1¼ cups chicken stock

1 tsp dried Mexican oregano

8 green New Mexico chillies, roasted, peeled and finely chopped (or, for more heat, use a few Serrano chillies, or Jalapeño and Anaheim)

sea salt and black pepper

Heat the oil in a saucepan over medium heat. Add the onion and fry for 2–3 minutes until softened. Add the garlic and fry for a further 1 minute. Stir in the flour and cumin and continue to cook for 3 minutes, stirring frequently. Gradually add the stock, stirring constantly, then bring the mixture to a simmer.

Add the oregano and cook for 30 minutes, or until the sauce begins to thicken. Add the chillies, stir well and cook for 5 minutes. Season, then blend using a stick blender, if you like, or serve in a more chunky form. This sauce is always served hot and is generally made fresh every day.

Hot tip: Use this as a breakfast sauce for eggs and fried potato, on tacos, or even with chilli nachos.

HOT & SWEET CHILLI DIPPING SAUCE

This is a delightful sauce with strong savoury flavours. If you are feeling adventurous, try adding a tablespoonful of the sauce when making lentil soup, or mixing it with grated cheese before making a cheese and ham toasted sandwich. It is popular with spicy pizza too!

2 tbsp white wine vinegar

110 g/generous ½ cup sugar

120 g/4¼ oz. ripe red sweet/bell peppers, deseeded and finely chopped

5 cm/2 inches fresh ginger, peeled and grated

1–2 Habanero chillies, deseeded and finely chopped

juice of ½ lime, or to taste

zest of 1 lemon

a good pinch of sea salt

¼ tsp fennel seeds

a good pinch of ground coriander

a good pinch of ground cumin

Pour the vinegar and 2 tablespoons water into a medium saucepan. Heat gently, then add the sugar and stir until it has dissolved. Add the red peppers, ginger and chillies. Continue to heat until the mixture comes to a gentle boil, stirring regularly.

Add the remaining ingredients, mix well and continue to cook for about 30 minutes, or until the mixture has reduced and thickened. Carefully taste – it will be hot! Season with a little more salt, if required, and perhaps a squeeze more of lime juice. Pour into a sterilized jar, seal and cool. Store in a cool, dark place. Do not refrigerate, as this can cause the sauce to crystallize. Serve at room temperature as a spicy sweet dip.

Hot tip: Use this to serve with fish cakes or spring rolls, or as a marinade for salmon steaks.

CHILLI BARBECUE BASTE

Basting involves periodically coating a piece of meat or fish with a sauce, marinade and/or its own juices as it cooks. It is an excellent technique for cooking on a barbecue, and this sauce provides flavour and a subtle heat that builds up over the cooking time. Equally, the butter that is the base of this recipe helps to replace the moisture that evaporates from the meat as it cooks. The end result should be succulent meat with a spicy, caramelized coating – exactly what we want from a barbecue.

125 g/1 stick salted butter

juice of 1 lemon

2 tsp muscovado/molasses sugar

2 garlic cloves, finely chopped

1 tsp tomato purée/paste

½ tsp dried oregano

1 tbsp Worcestershire sauce

1 tbsp hot sauce, such as Trees Can't Dance Flaming Lips Hot Sauce

sea salt and black pepper

Gently heat the butter in a medium saucepan over medium heat until it melts. Add the lemon juice and bring to a very gentle simmer, being careful not to burn the butter.

Add the sugar and stir until it dissolves. Add the garlic and tomato purée and gently cook, being careful once again not to burn the butter or the garlic. Add the oregano, Worcestershire sauce and hot sauce. Remove from the heat, season with salt and pepper and use immediately.

Hot tip: Use this to baste chicken, pork or veggie dishes while they cook, or to coat meat, fish or vegetable kebabs/kabobs before they are barbecued.

ROASTED PEPPER & CARAMELIZED ONION RELISH

Relishes are often categorized as either ketchup-based (for burgers) or mustard-based (for hotdogs). They can be sweet, savoury, spicy, mild, sharp or even sour. In fact the classic American 'relishes' actually refer to dill-pickled mini cucumbers/gherkins that were traditionally served as a side to a burger. Relishes originate in India, and were born out of the necessity to preserve fresh fruit and vegetables. This recipe is the root of one of my favourite chilli sauces, but it started life as a relish recipe. Rather than using the conventional tomato base, it uses roasted sweet peppers, whose natural sweetness balances very well with the acidity of the vinegar. The result is sweet, sour and spicy – perfect with slightly smoky burgers.

2 ripe Romano-style red sweet/bell peppers

2 tbsp sunflower oil

1 large onion, diced

2 garlic cloves, crushed

2 tbsp cider vinegar

1 tbsp red wine vinegar

2 tbsp brown sugar

2–3 red Jalapeño chillies (or other red chillies), chopped

1 tbsp tomato purée/paste

2 tsp Cajun spice blend

½ tsp paprika (use Pimentón Dulce if you want a smoky-flavoured relish)

Put the peppers on a baking sheet and put under a hot grill/broiler. When the skin has blackened on top, turn them over and repeat the process. Once all the skin is charred, turn off the grill/broiler and put the peppers into a medium food bag. Seal the top and set aside to cool. When cool, peel the charred skins away from the flesh and deseed the peppers. Roughly dice the roasted pepper flesh.

Heat the oil in a medium heavy-based saucepan over medium-high heat and fry the onion for 10–15 minutes until caramelized. Stir frequently to prevent it from burning. When it has a nice golden colour, add the garlic and fry for 30 seconds–1 minute, or until softened and golden. Add the peppers, both types of vinegar and the sugar. Bring to the boil, stirring constantly to dissolve the sugar (you can add a splash of water if needed). Reduce the heat and stir in the chillies, tomato purée/paste, Cajun spice and paprika. Add 100 ml/scant ½ cup of water and return to a simmer. Cook for 10–15 minutes, stirring regularly and adding a little more water if required, until rich and thick. Adding little and often, and only if really needed, is best, as we want the end relish to be rich, thick and sticky. Pour straight into a sterilized jar and seal. Leave to cool. Store in the fridge once opened.

Hot tip: Use this with homemade burgers; it's also perfect with chipotle beef, lamb or chicken, or with veggie dishes. For a hot, smoky relish, reduce the fresh chilli content and add a generous teaspoon of crushed Chipotle chilli. For a delicious North African relish, to serve with lamb burgers, substitute Jordanian Baharat Blend (see page 68) for the Cajun spice blend and add 3–4 finely chopped sun-dried apricots.

6
INDIA

NOTED CHILLIES

Kashmiri, Pusa Jawala (pictured opposite, right), Naga Jolokia, Naga Morich (pictured opposite, left), Lal Mirch (red chilli), Guntur.

CHILLI FACTS & FICTION

In Northern India, dried ground Naga chillies are used to deter marauding wild elephants. The elephant's olfactory sense is so acute that this powdered chilli causes it immediate discomfort if it sniffs even the tiniest amount.

A combination of chillies and lemons are hung above the entrance to a house to deter evil.

SRI LANKAN DARK ROAST CURRY PASTE

The flavour and appearance of this paste rely on the spices being well toasted, but if any are burnt they will ruin the final result. Make sure each spice is beginning to colour but that none have been singed on the pan. To do this, it is ideal to keep the seeds moving as they toast.

5 tbsp coriander seeds

5-cm/2-inch stick cinnamon, broken into pieces

½ tsp cloves

4 tsp cumin seeds

2 tsp fennel seeds

1 tsp fenugreek seeds

½ tsp cardamom seeds

8 large dried red chillies, deseeded

1 tbsp nut oil

2 large garlic cloves

2.5-cm/1-inch piece fresh ginger, peeled and chopped

2-cm/¾-inch piece lemongrass, tough outer leaves removed, chopped

2 tbsp coconut milk

2 tbsp cider vinegar

1 tbsp lime juice

Put the coriander, cinnamon and cloves in a heavy-based saucepan and toast over medium heat until they begin to darken and release their aromas, shaking the pan frequently. Remove from the pan and toast the remaining spice seeds in the same way. Allow to cool and grind to a fine powder using a grinder or pestle and mortar.

Put all the spices in a food processor or blender with the chillies and oil. Blend together, adding the garlic, ginger and lemongrass, and gradually adding the coconut milk, vinegar and lime juice to make a smooth, fragrant paste. Loosen with a little water if required. Blend until you have a smooth and glossy paste.

Store in an airtight container in the fridge. It will happily keep for several weeks like this.

Hot tip: Use this to make a delicious prawn/shrimp curry.

SOUR FISH CURRY PASTE

I often make this particular paste and love the buttery-ness the fenugreek imparts to the final curry, perfect with the sourness of the kokum or tamarind. The little hint of aniseed that fennel seeds give is virtually indispensable in fish curries.

1 tsp fenugreek seeds

1 tsp mustard seeds

½ tsp fennel seeds

8–10 red chillies, deseeded and chopped

1 tsp sea salt

2 pieces kokum, soaked in warm water to soften (or 1 tsp unsweetened tamarind paste)

6 garlic cloves, peeled and chopped

10 curry leaves

1 shallot, chopped

3 tbsp vegetable oil

1 tsp ground turmeric

Put the fenugreek, mustard and fennel seeds in a saucepan and toast until the mustard seeds start to pop. Set aside to cool, then grind to a fine powder using a grinder or a pestle and mortar.

Put the chillies, salt, kokum, garlic, curry leaves and shallot into a blender, then process, adding the vegetable oil while mixing. Add the ground spices and the turmeric, and give everything a final blitz to ensure an even mix.

Hot tip: Use this to make the perfect fish curry; ideal with monkfish. This also works very well with chicken.

VINDALOO CURRY PASTE

A vindaloo is still something of a maligned curry – a joke dish that is too hot to be enjoyed and only eaten by the foolish and/or drunk. The reality, however, is very different. It is one of the most finely flavoured curries you can make and, although often very hot, it is rarely uncomfortably so. This paste is my absolute favourite of the many (many) I have made, and it works equally well with pork, lamb or even beef. I would definitely recommend making it at least 24 hours in advance of using it, to get the best flavour. I have kept it in a sealed pot in my fridge for weeks, and it only improves over time. My top tips are: take a few spoonfuls to marinate the meat for a few hours before actually cooking the curry; use more onions than you think you need (ensuring you get some colour into them by frying before adding the other ingredients); and slow cook it, if you have time – 24 hours at around 80°C (175°F) is about perfect.

1 tsp cumin seeds

5 cloves

5-cm/2-inch piece cinnamon stick, roughly broken

8 black peppercorns

1 green cardamom pod

¼ piece star anise

1 tsp black onion seeds

3-cm/1¼-inch piece fresh ginger, peeled and roughly chopped

6 large garlic cloves, peeled

1 tbsp unsweetened tamarind paste

5 tsp cider vinegar

4 tbsp plus 1 tsp vegetable oil

10–20 chillies, deseeded, such as a mixture of green Finger chillies and red Bird's Eyes, to taste

Put the cumin seeds in a heavy-based pan over medium heat and add the cloves, cinnamon, peppercorns, cardamom and star anise. Lightly toast the spices, shaking the pan frequently. Allow to cool slightly. Remove the seeds from the cardamom pod and put into a spice grinder. Add the other roasted ingredients and the onion seeds, and grind into a coarse powder. (Alternatively, use a pestle and mortar.)

Put the ginger and garlic into a mini food processor and add the tamarind, vinegar, oil and chillies. Tip in the ground spices and blitz into a smooth paste. Pack the mixture into a container and seal tightly. Put into the fridge and allow to mature for at least 24 hours before using.

Hot tip: Use this to marinate pork, lamb, beef or vegetables before cooking.

SAMBAR POWDER

Full of delicious southern Indian flavours, this powder can be added to any dish. It's great in soups or for flavouring vegetarian dishes.

10 dried red chillies

4 tbsp coriander seeds

2 tbsp cumin seeds

2 tsp fenugreek seeds

2 tsp black peppercorns

1 tsp black onion seeds

2 tsp toovar dal (pigeon peas)

2 tsp chana dal (yellow split peas)

2 tsp urad dal (split black gram)

20 dried curry leaves

2 tsp ground turmeric

1 tsp ground asafoetida

Put the chillies in heavy-based saucepan over medium heat and add the coriander, cumin, fenugreek seeds, peppercorns and onion seeds. Toast the spices until they begin to release their aromas, shaking the pan frequently.

Tip the spices into a bowl and repeat the same process with the dals, being careful not let them burn. Tip them into the bowl with the spices, then transfer them all to a spice grinder or mortar, add the curry leaves and grind to a fairly fine powder. Stir in the turmeric and asafoetida. Transfer to an airtight container and store in cool dark place until you are ready to use it.

Hot tip: Use this to flavour lentils or to thicken a spicy sauce.

XACUTI CURRY POWDER

This recipe originates from Goa and, as such, is strongly associated with the fine seafood curries of that coastline. It has a distinct hint of aniseed from the star anise and the fennel seeds, which balance beautifully with the sweetness of the coconut and the warmth of the chillies.

120 g/1⅓ cups desiccated/unsweetened shredded coconut (or flesh from ½ fresh coconut, grated)

6–8 red Kashmiri chillies, deseeded

6 cloves

1 star anise

5-cm/2-inch piece cinnamon stick, broken up

1 tsp black peppercorns

1 tsp cumin seeds

1 tbsp coriander seeds

¼ tsp fenugreek seeds

1 tsp fennel seeds

1 tbsp poppy seeds

4–5 dried garlic flakes

1 tsp ground turmeric

½ tsp grated nutmeg

¼ tsp ground ginger

Heat a heavy-based frying pan/skillet over medium heat. If you are using fresh coconut, toast this in the pan first until it just begins to colour around the edges. Brush out into a bowl and set aside. Return the pan to the heat and add the chillies, cloves, star anise, cinnamon, peppercorns, cumin, coriander, fenugreek and fennel seeds. Toast for a few minutes until they begin to release their aromas. Add the poppy seeds (and desiccated coconut, if you are using this) and toast for a further 1–2 minutes. Allow to cool then put into a spice grinder along with the fresh coconut, if using, and the dried garlic. Blitz to a fine powder and then stir in the turmeric, nutmeg and ginger.

To make this as a paste: replace the matching dry ingredients with the following fresh ones: fresh coconut, 4–5 garlic cloves and a 2.5-cm/1-inch piece of fresh ginger. When blending, add 1 tablespoon of vegetable oil to the mix and add water as required to achieve your preferred paste consistency.

Hot tip: This recipe works particularly well with crab, fish or prawns/shrimp, although it can easily be used with chicken or to create a delicious vegetarian curry. Use this with a little water to make a paste and add to frying onions to create the flavouring sauce for a great seafood curry.

NEPALESE SEKUWA MARINADE

Marinating in yogurt is traditional throughout the Middle East and Asia. The process of fermenting the milk turns the yogurt acidic and so it acts to tenderize meat in the same way that a vinegar- or citrus-based marinade would and tends to produce really juicy and flavoursome results.

1 tbsp cumin seeds

1 tsp coriander seeds

1 tsp black peppercorns

¼ tsp Szechuan pepper

1 tsp sea salt, or to taste

½ tsp ground turmeric

1 large onion, finely chopped

2–3 celery sticks, chopped

3 red Bird's Eye chillies

2 garlic cloves

2-cm/¾-inch piece fresh ginger, peeled and sliced

juice of ½ lemon

2 tbsp mustard oil

1 tbsp soy sauce

500 ml/2 cups plain/natural yogurt

a small bunch of coriander/cilantro or dill, chopped

Put the cumin and coriander seeds in a heavy-based saucepan over medium heat and lightly toast, shaking the pan frequently. Tip into a mortar or spice grinder and add the peppercorns, Szechuan pepper and salt. Grind well, then stir in the turmeric.

Put all the spices into a food processor or blender with the onion, celery, chillies, garlic and ginger. Pulse a few times to roughly blend. Add the lemon juice, oil and soy sauce, and blend into a smooth paste. Tip into a bowl and stir in the yogurt and coriander.

Hot tip: Use this for chicken or lamb skewers.

JALFREZI PASTE

2 tsp white cumin seeds

1 tsp pink peppercorns

1 tsp mustard seeds

1 tsp fenugreek seeds

1 tsp coriander seeds

1 cardamom pod

2 cloves

2 large garlic cloves, peeled

5-cm/2-inch piece fresh ginger, peeled and roughly chopped

½ tsp sea salt

juice of ½ lemon

2 tbsp groundnut oil

2 tbsp tomato purée/paste

1 tsp ground turmeric

2 Bird's Eye chillies, deseeded and chopped

1 hot green chilli, deseeded and chopped

a small bunch of coriander/cilantro, finely chopped

A dish that originated in China but is now a Bengali classic, the jalfrezi is a strongly flavoured, dry curry. I like to add a few sliced fresh green chillies to the final curry towards the end of cooking.

Put the cumin seeds in a heavy-based saucepan over medium heat and add the peppercorns, mustard seeds, fenugreek seeds, coriander seeds, cardamom and cloves. Toast gently until the mustard seeds start to pop, shaking the pan frequently to prevent scorching. Allow to cool slightly, then remove the cardamom seeds from the pod and discard the husk. Grind these toasted spices and the cardamom seeds with a mortar and pestle or spice grinder until you have a fairly fine powder.

Put the ground spices into a mini food processor or mortar and add the garlic, ginger and salt, then blitz or pound to break them down. Add the lemon juice, oil and tomato purée and pound/blitz to a smooth paste. Add the turmeric and both types of chillies and continue to pound/blitz until smooth. Finally, add the coriander and mix well.

Pack into an airtight container and store in the fridge until you are ready to use it.

Hot tip: Use this to cook with chicken, prawns/shrimp or vegetables.

KASHMIRI LAMB MARINADE

Kashmiri chillies are slightly less pungent than the majority of chillies found in north Indian food. They are bred to have a very fine distinctive flavour and to add vibrant colour to any dish. The beauty of their slightly less intense heat is that you can add a significant number to virtually any dish, getting all the benefits of their great flavour and colour without making the resulting dish unpleasantly hot. For this dish, it is necessary to prepare them and make them into a powder.

2 tsp Kashmiri chilli powder (or flakes)

¼ tsp ground cardamom

1 tsp garam masala

1 tsp sea salt flakes, or to taste

120 g/½ cup full-fat plain/natural yogurt

2.5-cm/1-inch piece fresh ginger, peeled and very finely chopped

2 garlic cloves, peeled and crushed

a small handful of coriander/cilantro leaves and stalks, finely chopped

a squeeze of lemon juice

Put the chilli powder in a medium bowl and add the other dry spices and the salt. Pour in the yogurt and stir well. Add the ginger, garlic and coriander, and mix together thoroughly. Add a little more salt to taste, if required, and a good squeeze of lemon juice. Cover and leave in the fridge for 1 hour for the flavours to mingle.

Hot tip: Use this to marinate lamb or chicken.

BENGALI KASUNDI (MUSTARD & CHILLI RELISH)

There are many ways to prepare the Indian relish, Kasundi, but it always contains mustard seeds – usually soaked in vinegar – and chillies. The first of the variations here was supplied to me by the incredible Simon Majumdar, whose legendary travels and knowledge make it a classic.

100 g/⅓ cup yellow mustard seeds

100 ml/scant ½ cup palm vinegar

4 green Finger chillies, deseeded and finely chopped

4 large garlic cloves, finely chopped

5-cm/2-inch piece fresh ginger, peeled and chopped

1 tsp sugar

a good squeeze of lime juice

vegetable oil, as needed (optional)

zest of ½ lime

SIMON'S KASUNDI *(opposite, top)*

Put the mustard seeds in a heavy-based saucepan over medium heat and toast until they begin to pop, shaking the pan frequently to avoid scorching any of the seeds. Remove from the pan and set aside to cool. Soak the mustard seeds in the palm vinegar, preferably overnight, then drain and reserve the vinegar.

Put the mustard seeds in a food processor or blender with the chillies, garlic, ginger, sugar and lime juice. Blend until you have a smooth paste. Add a little of the reserved vinegar, or some oil or water, if required, to aid blending. (Using water or oil will impact on the amount of time the finished product can be kept, so if you plan to make a larger batch and store it, use vinegar.) Add the lime zest and stir thoroughly. Transfer to a sterilized jar with an airtight lid and store in the fridge until required. It will keep for about 2 weeks.

4 tbsp vegetable oil

1 tbsp yellow mustard seeds

1 tbsp black mustard seeds

1 tsp cumin seeds

1 tsp coriander seeds

4 garlic cloves

5-cm/2-inch piece fresh ginger

4 hot green Finger chillies, finely chopped

100 ml/scant ½ cup cider vinegar

1 tsp ground turmeric

4 large ripe tomatoes

2 tsp sugar

2 tsp sea salt

VARIATION 1 *(opposite, bottom left)*

A 'cooked' Kasundi that incorporates fresh tomatoes. Pour into a jar when hot for the best keeping properties.

Heat the oil in a heavy-based saucepan over medium heat. Add both types of mustard seed, the cumin and coriander and gently fry for about 4–5 minutes stirring constantly. Add the garlic, ginger, chillies and vinegar, and cook for another 4–5 minutes. Stir in the turmeric, tomatoes, sugar and salt. Bring to a simmer and cook for a further 10–15 minutes until the contents of the pan have reduced and thickened. With a stick blender or in a food processor blend the contents of the pan into a smooth paste. Transfer to a sterilized container while still hot, seal and store in the fridge.

2 tbsp yellow mustard seeds, soaked
for 24 hours in cider vinegar

5 small hot red chillies, deseeded
and roughly chopped

3 garlic cloves, crushed

1 small green mango, peeled and
roughly chopped

1 tsp sugar

sea salt

VARIATION 2 *(above, right)*

Another 'raw' Kasundi with the added fruitiness of green mango.

Put all the ingredients into a food processor or blender and process until
you have a smooth paste. Season as required with salt. Transfer to an airtight
container and store in the fridge until required.

Hot tip: Use any of these in sandwiches, with your favourite curry, or with
spicy beef dishes.

PYAJ KO ACHAR (NEPALESE ONION CHUTNEY) *(below, left)*

Achars are fresh chutneys. They are easy to make, taste delicious and look attractive at the table. They come in an unending array of styles and use an equally extensive range of cooking methods.

2 tbsp vegetable oil

2 red onions, peeled and chopped

6 garlic cloves, peeled and roughly chopped

2 tbsp chana dal

2 hot red chillies, stalks removed, chopped

1 tsp tamarind paste (or a good squeeze of lemon juice)

1 tbsp yellow mustard seeds

a pinch of fenugreek seeds

a pinch of dried thyme

2 fresh curry leaves, torn

sea salt

Heat 1 tablespoon of the oil in a heavy-based saucepan over medium heat and fry the onions, garlic, dal and chillies until the onions have taken on a golden colour. Remove from the heat and spoon into a mortar, then add the tamarind paste and a good seasoning of salt. Pound this mixture using a pestle. This process will take some time! Once this is smooth, scrape it out into a serving bowl.

Wipe out the pan and heat the remaining oil over medium heat. Add the mustard seeds and fenugreek and cook until the mustard seeds start to pop. Add the thyme and curry leaves, and cook for 15 seconds. Pour this oil over the other ingredients in the serving bowl.

Hot tip: Use this as a dip for homemade roti or flatbreads, or raw vegetables.

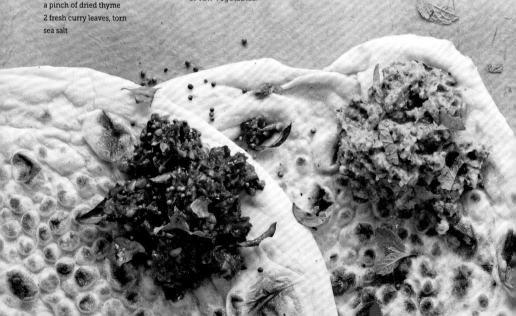

BABARI KO ACHAR (MINT & CHILLI CHUTNEY)

(opposite, right)

A fresh, fiery, minty dip from Nepal/Northern India, this is an ideal complement to the onion chutney opposite. Great with flatbreads or with spicy marinated meat kebabs/kabobs.

a large handful of mint, roughly chopped

2 green chillies, such as Jalapeños, deseeded and roughly chopped

1 red onion, roughly chopped

3 garlic cloves, roughly chopped

2.5-cm/1-inch piece fresh ginger, peeled and finely chopped

125 g/½ cup plain/natural yogurt

juice of 1 lemon

sea salt

Put the mint, chillies, onion, garlic and ginger into a food processor or blender and pulse together. Add the yogurt and continue to blend into a smooth paste. Scrape down the sides of the blender as required, to ensure an even mix. Add the lemon juice and pulse to combine. Season with salt to taste. Transfer to a bowl and serve. If covered, it can be stored in the fridge for a few days until required, but always bring it to room temperature before serving.

Hot tip: Use this to serve with tandoori trout, rotis and fresh, crunchy salad.

SABSE BORANI

Although originally designed to be served as sour yogurt drinks, Sabse recipes make delicious dips, and this recipe from Afghanistan is no exception.

250 g/1 cup plain/natural yogurt

a large handful of spinach

2 tbsp vegetable oil

1 onion, finely chopped

2 garlic cloves, very finely chopped

1 tsp hot chilli powder (Naga powder, if you dare)

a squeeze of lemon juice

sea salt and black pepper

2–3 mint leaves, to garnish

Put the yogurt in muslin/cheesecloth and suspend over a bowl. Leave for 1 hour or until any excess moisture has drained away, squeezing the muslin occasionally. Heat a saucepan over medium heat. Add 2 tablespoons water and the spinach leaves. Reduce the heat, cover and allow the spinach to wilt, then remove from the heat, drain and set aside.

Heat the oil in a frying pan/skillet over medium heat. Add the onion and fry, stirring constantly, until it is evenly golden brown but not burnt. Add a little water to the pan if required. Add the garlic and chilli powder and fry for a further 2 minutes. Stir in the spinach and cook for a further minute. Remove from the heat and allow to cool to room temperature.

Put the onion and spinach mixture in a small bowl and add the yogurt. Stir well until they are thoroughly mixed. Season to taste with salt and pepper. Squeeze the lemon juice over the dip and garnish with fresh mint leaves. Serve at room temperature.

Hot tip: Use this mixed with spiced grilled/broiled fish in a flatbread.

7
ASIA

NOTED CHILLIES

Thai Dragon (pictured opposite, above), Bird's Eye, Chi-Chen, Cayenne, Goat's Horn, Japone, Tears of Fire, Shishito (pictured opposite, below), Takanotsume, Japone, Chi-Chen, Hainan Yellow Lantern and Facing Heaven (still commercially grown in China!).

CHILLI FACTS & FICTION

In a recent field test, identical chilli seeds were planted in Indonesia, China, India and Thailand. The fruit from the Indonesian plants were consistently the hottest although, interestingly, in a consumer survey conducted at the same time 'pungency' was not the main consideration for Indonesians in general. Perhaps, though, this was because it didn't need to be a consideration!

Not surprisingly, chillies are regularly used in traditional medicine in China. Research there has shown success in treating conditions such as angina and high blood pressure.

THAI GREEN CURRY PASTE

The key to a good Thai curry of any description is the paste. These pastes are best made using a large and heavy pestle and mortar because it makes the task of pounding the ingredients much easier. By pounding each ingredient to a pulp, you get a smoother and more homogenized paste – the individual ingredients are actually transformed into a single entity. If you use a food processor, no matter how good it is, it is simply cutting the ingredients into smaller and smaller pieces. This does little to actually combine them and leads to a more 'bitty' and granular paste. Also, because of the way Thai pastes are subsequently cooked in coconut milk rather than fried in oil they have less opportunity to soften and blend during the cooking process. The traditional process prepares them perfectly for how they are intended to be cooked.

3–4 lemongrass stalks, tough outer leaves discarded, chopped

2-cm/¾-inch piece fresh red turmeric, chopped

10 medium-hot green Thai chillies, deseeded and finely chopped

10 hot green chillies, such as Bird's Eye, deseeded and chopped

2 red shallots, finely sliced

4–5 large garlic cloves, chopped

5–6 frozen makrut lime leaves (or dried), finely chopped

5-cm/2-inch piece fresh galangal root, peeled and chopped

2-cm/¾-inch piece fresh coriander/cilantro root, chopped

1 tsp Thai shrimp paste (gapi)

sea salt and white pepper

Starting with the lemongrass, work through the ingredients list in order. Using a mortar and pestle, pound each ingredient to a smooth paste before adding the next. It is time-consuming and hard work, but the end result is significantly better than a paste made using a food processor.

If stored in an airtight container, this paste will keep for up to 4 weeks in the fridge, although it is better made fresh as required.

Hot tip: Use this to make the perfect chicken or seafood green curry.

THAI RED CURRY PASTE

A good Thai red curry paste requires patience and commitment to make well. This is obviously great to make curries with, but I would also recommend it as the key flavouring ingredient for Thai fish cakes. It adds a citrusy little kick and the shrimp paste helps to enhance the flavour of the fish.

1 tsp white peppercorns

2 tsp coriander seeds

1 tsp cumin seeds

4 cloves

½ tsp grated nutmeg

2 small lemongrass stalks, tough outer leaves discarded, chopped

10 red chillies, deseeded and chopped

2 tsp makrut lime zest (available frozen) (or zest of 1 small lime)

2 red shallots, chopped

5–6 garlic cloves, finely chopped

a small handful of coriander/cilantro leaves and stalks, chopped

½ tsp shrimp paste (gapi)

¼ tsp sea salt

Put the peppercorns in a saucepan over medium heat and add the coriander seeds, cumin seeds and cloves. Toast until they release their aromas, shaking the pan frequently. Remove from the heat and allow to cool. Using a pestle and mortar, grind the spices to a fine powder. Pour into a small bowl, stir in the nutmeg and set aside.

Take each fresh ingredient in turn and pound it in the mortar into a smooth paste. Ensure that each ingredient is fully broken down before adding the next. Once you have achieved a smooth consistency, scrape the mixture into a small bowl and mix in the finely ground dry spices. Store in an airtight container in the fridge.

Hot tip: Use this to cook with chicken, duck, tofu or vegetables, or to flavour Thai fish cakes.

MUSSAMAN CURRY PASTE

10 long red dried Thai chillies, deseeded

4 tbsp finely chopped red shallots

4 tbsp finely chopped garlic cloves

2 tbsp finely chopped fresh galangal

1 tbsp finely chopped fresh ginger

2 tbsp finely chopped fresh lemongrass (tough outer leaves removed)

2 tsp finely chopped coriander/cilantro root

1 tsp cumin seeds

1 tbsp coriander seeds

4 cloves

5 black peppercorns

3 cardamom pods

2 small pieces of mace

a small piece of cassia bark (optional)

½ tsp sea salt

1 tbsp salted roasted peanuts

1 tsp palm sugar

a little vegetable oil, if needed

This is perhaps the most famous of all the Thai curry pastes. To make a good mussaman, what seems like an industrial quantity of paste is required. With this in mind it is easier to measure the ingredients by the tablespoon rather than by specifying a number of garlic cloves or lemongrass stalks. The curry originated in Persia but was quickly absorbed into Thai cuisine where it now holds an almost legendary significance. It has become increasingly elaborate over the last few centuries.

Soak the chillies in hot water for 30 minutes. Drain them and squeeze out any excess moisture. Roughly chop the chillies, then put them into a saucepan over low heat and add the shallots, garlic, galangal, ginger, lemongrass and coriander root. Roast for a few moments (adding a little water, if required) until they begin to brown and become aromatic. Put these ingredients into a mortar and use a pestle to pound them into a smooth paste.

Put the cumin seeds, coriander seeds, cloves, peppercorns, cardamom, mace and cassia bark (if using) in a frying pan/skillet. Toast for a few minutes until they become fragrant, shaking the pan frequently. Allow to cool slightly, then remove the seeds from the cardamom pods and discard the husk. Put the toasted seeds into a clean mortar or a spice grinder and grind to a fine powder.

Add the salt to the lemongrass mixture and continue to pound in the mortar, then add the peanuts and pound further. Sift in the ground dry spices to remove any larger pieces. Add the sugar and continue to pound until you have a smooth, rich paste. Add a little vegetable oil, if necessary, in order to loosen the mixture. Cover and set aside until you are ready to cook.

Hot tip: Use this to make a chicken or beef curry.

NAM PRIK PAO *(below, left)*

Whether this is actually a cooking paste, a condiment, a dip or even a jam is a matter of conjecture, but it clearly illustrates the flexibility of the flavours and the many uses to which Nam Prik Pao lends itself. It is delicious with rice, noodles, vegetables, fish and meat.

120 ml/½ cup vegetable oil

3 large shallots, chopped

3 garlic cloves, chopped

a pinch of sea salt

3 Thai chillies, deseeded and roughly chopped

½ tsp shrimp paste (gapi)

2 tbsp ground dried shrimp

1½ tbsp fish sauce, or to taste

2 tsp palm sugar, or to taste

1 tsp tamarind paste, or to taste

Heat a small wok over medium heat and add 2 tbsp of the oil. Fry the shallots and garlic for 5 minutes, or until softened and translucent. Put them into a mortar and pound with a pestle into a smooth paste. Add the salt and chillies and repeat the process. Add the shrimp paste and dried shrimp. Continue pounding until you have a fine, uniform paste.

Put the remaining oil in the wok and heat over medium heat. Reduce the heat and add the paste. Fry gently to allow the ingredients to combine their flavours. Season with the fish sauce, palm sugar and tamarind paste to taste. Mix well and remove from the heat.

Store in an airtight sterilized container in the fridge.

Hot tip: Use this in stir-fries, as a dip for homemade pork crackling or in classic Thai Tom Yam Gung soup.

'SOUR ORANGE' CURRY PASTE *(opposite, right)*

Unlike the sour orange pastes and marinades of Central America, this Thai curry paste is so called because of its colour, not because of the presence of sour oranges. Thai pastes are generally pounded together in a mortar beginning with the ingredients that will take the most work to reduce to a pulp, then adding further ingredients in a logical sequence until everything is reduced to a smooth paste. They are simple to make, although often time consuming and a little tiring! However, the individual characteristics this method produces make up for the extra effort. You could, of course, decide to blitz everything together in a blender, and this would produce a very delicious and usable version of a Thai paste, but I would urge you to do it the hard way at least once. The difference can be astonishing. It is worth remembering two things: the larger and heavier the pestle and mortar you use the easier the process will be; and a good wrist technique will always produce better results more quickly than using brute force.

5–6 dried long red Cayenne-style chillies, deseeded and soaked in warm water or vinegar for 20 minutes

3 whole dried red Bird's Eye chillies, stalks removed

½ tsp sea salt

1 lemongrass stalk, tough outer leaves removed, finely chopped

2 Bird's Eye chillies, deseeded and chopped

1 large or 2 small red shallots, finely chopped

1 tsp shrimp paste

1 tsp tamarind paste

Remove the chillies from their soaking liquid and squeeze out the excess moisture, then chop finely. Heat a small frying pan/skillet over medium heat and briefly toast the dried Bird's Eye chillies until they just begin to colour.

Put the Cayenne chillies and dried Bird's Eye chillies into a mortar and add the salt. Using a pestle, pound the chillies until they have formed a smooth paste. Add the lemongrass and repeat the process. Do this with each ingredient in turn, making sure you have a smooth paste before adding the next ingredient.

The finished paste will be very hot, sour and vividly coloured.

Hot tip: Use this with coconut milk, fish sauce and palm sugar to make the perfect hot Thai curry sauce for white fish.

NUOC CHAM, HO CHI MINH-STYLE *(below, left)*

My version of Nuoc Cham has evolved to incorporate some wonderful flavours, ending up as a southern Vietnamese version of Nuoc Cham and is particularly good with beef and noodle salads.

1 small lime

2 garlic cloves, crushed

2.5-cm/1-inch piece fresh ginger, peeled and very finely chopped

2 small hot green chillies, deseeded and finely chopped

50 ml/scant ¼ cup coconut water

2 tsp unrefined (golden caster) sugar

2 tbsp Vietnamese-style fish sauce (or Thai fish sauce, to taste)

Squeeze the juice from the lime into a small bowl and set aside. Scrape the pulp from the lime into a mortar. Add the garlic, ginger and chillies and pound, using a pestle, to form a paste. If you find it difficult to pound this to a paste the ingredients could be briefly pulsed in a food processor to achieve the desired consistency.

Add the coconut water and sugar to the bowl of lime juice and stir to dissolve the sugar. Scrape the paste into the bowl with the lime juice mixture, add the fish sauce and mix well. (Vietnamese fish sauce is lighter in style than traditional nam pla – Thai fish sauce. If you are unable to source the Vietnamese sauce, Thai-style fish sauce works well, but you may wish to reduce the quantity slightly or add it gradually to taste.)

Hot tip: Use this to flavour noodles, grilled beef, rice and salads.

TUONG GOI CUON (VIETNAMESE PEANUT SAUCE) *(opposite, right)*

Possibly, Tuong Goi Cuon is the perfect dipping sauce for serving with spring rolls. The recipe itself is incredibly simple, but it can be embellished in many ways to suit your personal taste. A truly authentic recipe in its simplest form uses water and vinegar with crushed peanuts added at the end; however, I think the finest version I have ever tasted uses pork stock instead of water, with tamarind as a souring agent instead of vinegar, and 1–2 tablespoons of peanut butter to every 4 tablespoons of hoisin! The point is, I am not convinced that these recipes should be set in stone. I think that making subtle changes and trying your own ideas reinvigorates recipes and can produce wonderful new tastes. It is good to start with an authentic recipe, but where you finally end up is part of the joy of cooking. This is the sauce I like!

180 ml/¾ cup warm pork stock, such as the cooking liquor from boiling a ham (or water)

4 tbsp hoisin sauce

1–2 tbsp peanut butter

2 tbsp tamarind paste or vinegar, plus extra tamarind for seasoning, if needed

2 tsp soy sauce

½ tsp cornflour/ cornstarch

1 tbsp vegetable oil

1 red shallot, finely chopped

4 garlic cloves, 3 finely chopped and 1 crushed

1 hot red chilli, such as Thai or Bird's Eye, deseeded and finely chopped

a pinch of palm sugar, if needed

Vietnamese fish sauce, if needed, or to taste (or Thai fish sauce, to taste)

a small handful of roasted unsalted peanuts

Pour the stock into a small bowl and add the hoisin sauce, peanut butter, tamarind, soy sauce and cornflour. Combine well using a fork or chopsticks.

Heat the oil in a small frying pan/skillet over high heat and fry the shallot for 8 minutes, or until golden brown and crispy. (If you do not have a small frying pan you may need to use a little more oil to recreate the effect of deep-frying.) Remove the fried shallot and drain on paper towels.

Tip out most of the oil, leaving about 1 teaspoon in the pan, and put over medium heat. Add the 3 chopped garlic cloves and fry briefly until they just begin to colour, then stir in the chilli. While stirring the garlic mixture constantly, pour the contents of the small bowl into the pan, and continue stirring until the mixture comes to the boil. Remove from the heat and taste – the sauce should be slightly sweet, but sour and distinctly savoury too. Season with palm sugar to add sweetness, if needed, Vietnamese fish sauce, for saltiness (you will need less if using Thai fish sauce), and tamarind paste to increase the essential 'sour' element. Crush the peanuts in a mortar.

To serve, transfer the peanut sauce to a serving bowl and add the crushed garlic and peanuts. Stir well, then sprinkle with the fried shallots. Serve at room temperature.

Hot tip: Use this for dipping spring rolls, or with simple fish and rice dishes.

Sambals are very satisfying to make and provide a great flavour resource for impromptu dishes when you just don't know what you want to make! There are well over 300 different sambal recipes, just from Indonesia, so if you enjoy the process, there are many to experiment with – some cooked and some raw. These recipes are some of my favourites and suitably HOT!

SAMBAL BALADO
(opposite, left)

10 hot green chillies, thinly sliced

½ tsp sea salt

3 garlic cloves, finely chopped

2 shallots, finely chopped

1 red (or green) tomato, deseeded

juice of 1 lemon

1 tbsp vegetable oil

Put the chillies and salt in a mortar and grind using a pestle. Add each remaining ingredient individually (except the oil) and pound between additions to make a uniform and slightly chunky paste.

Heat the oil in a wok or frying pan/skillet and gently fry the paste until the ingredients are cooked through. They will lose their sharp, raw taste and the paste will become a little sweeter. Pour into a small bowl and allow to cool.

SAMBAL KACANG
(opposite, middle)

150 g/1¼ cups deep-fried peanuts (or roasted salted peanuts)

1 small shallot, finely chopped

2 garlic cloves, chopped

4 Bird's Eye chillies, deseeded and chopped

1 makrut lime leaf, finely chopped

2½ tbsp ketjap manis – sweet dark soy (or 2 tbsp dark soy sauce plus 1 tsp sugar)

½ tsp sea salt

500 ml/2 cups water

2 tsp lime juice

Put the peanuts in a mortar and grind using a pestle. Add the shallot and pound into a paste. Repeat with the garlic and chillies, making sure each forms a thick paste before adding the next.

Tip the paste into a saucepan and add the lime leaf, ketjap manis, salt and water. Bring to a gentle simmer and cook for 1 hour, stirring occasionally, or until most of the water has evaporated. Stir in the lime juice, then allow to cool and serve.

SAMBAL OELEK *(above, right)*

10 hot red chillies, such as Bird's Eye, stalks removed

½ tsp sea salt

½ tsp blachan shrimp paste

1 tbsp usweetened tamarind paste or lime juice

Put the chillies and salt in a large mortar and pound into a smooth purée with a pestle. Add the shrimp paste and continue to grind together until completely mixed. Add the tamarind and grind until you have a smooth red paste.

NASI GORENG SPICE PASTE & BLACHAN

Literally, Nasi Goreng means 'fried rice', and the dish is unofficially the national dish of Indonesia. Originally, it was a way of using up leftover rice and meat or fish, but it is now often used to describe even the most complex fried-rice dish. This paste provides the spicy flavouring that is the heart of any good nasi goreng dish. Blachan is a dark shrimp paste that is surprisingly easy to make. Below is a simple recipe if you want to try making your own.

25 g/¼ cup roasted salted peanuts

2 tbsp vegetable oil

4 large garlic cloves, roughly chopped

2 shallots, chopped

6 red chillies, roughly chopped

1 tsp blachan (dark shrimp paste, see below)

1 tsp salt

Put the peanuts in a food processor and briefly blitz them. Add the remaining ingredients and process until you have thick paste – be sure to scrape down the sides of the bowl to ensure everything is evenly mixed.

You can store this paste in an airtight container in the fridge, but it is better to make it fresh as required.

Hot tip: Use with any fried rice dish, or to coat chicken before cooking.

TO MAKE BLACHAN (IF YOU FANCY IT!)

100 g/3½ oz. dried shrimp powder

40 g/scant ½ cup desiccated coconut

2 small onions, chopped

5 garlic cloves, chopped

2.5-cm/1-inch piece fresh ginger, peeled and chopped

150 ml/scant ⅔ cup lemon juice

3 tsp chilli powder

sea salt

Toast the shrimp powder in a frying pan/skillet over low heat for about 1–2 minutes, stirring constantly – be careful not to allow the powder to burn. Pour into a bowl and allow to cool.

Briefly toast the desiccated coconut in the frying pan, stirring constantly, until it has turned a rich golden colour, being careful not to allow it to burn. Pour into a separate bowl to cool.

Put the remaining ingredients into a food processor or blender and blend to a thick, smooth paste. Add the shrimp paste and coconut, and continue to blend, adding a little water as required to make a thick paste. Season with salt to taste. Pack into an airtight container and store in the fridge.

MALAY CURRY POWDER

I must admit that I encountered this curry powder not in Malaysia but in Cape Town, South Africa. It was used as a dry rub for meat before being placed on the ubiquitous Braai. It is exceptionally good with fish and chicken, although it is also great as the base powder for my favourite pheasant and prune curry. I use this curry powder to make the sauce for Pinang Kerrie Sauce (see page 33).

3 dried red Bird's Eye chillies, deseeded

5-cm/2-inch piece cinnamon stick, roughly broken up

2 tsp Szechuan peppercorns

½ piece star anise

1 tsp coriander seeds

1 tsp fennel seeds

5 cloves

seeds from 1 green cardamom pod

2–3 dried makrut lime leaves, roughly broken up

a good grating of fresh nutmeg

2 tsp ground turmeric

Put the chillies in a heavy-based saucepan over medium heat and add the cinnamon, peppercorns, star anise, coriander seeds, fennel seeds and cloves. Toast until they begin to release their aroma. Add the cardamom seeds and toast for another 30 seconds.

Tip the toasted spices into a mortar or spice grinder. Add the lime leaves and grind to a fine powder. Tip into a bowl and add the nutmeg and turmeric, then mix together thoroughly. Transfer to a sealable container until you are ready to use it.

Hot tip: Use this to cook with fish or pheasant.

KOREAN CHILLI MARINADE FOR BEEF

In Korean restaurants, thin strips of beef are marinated, then cooked on hot coals at the table and often served with a fermented soy bean, chilli and rice condiment called gochujang.

2 tbsp sesame seeds

4 spring onions/scallions, sliced

2 green Finger chillies, thinly sliced diagonally

2 garlic cloves, very thinly sliced

5-cm/2-inch piece fresh ginger, peeled and finely chopped

4 tbsp dark soy sauce

1 tbsp nut oil

1 tbsp rice wine vinegar

2 tsp palm sugar

Put the sesame seeds in a small saucepan over medium heat and toast until lightly golden, shaking the pan frequently. Tip into a serving bowl and add the remaining ingredients. Combine thoroughly.

Hot tip: Use this as a marinade for thin strips of beef. The beef will need at least 1 hour to marinate.

KIMCHI  *(opposite)*

For my 38th birthday I was taken out in Glasgow for a proper night out. We ended up eating in an extremely authentic Korean restaurant. I am ashamed to say that it was my first real experience of Korean food, and to this day I can't really recall most of the dishes we ate, but it did introduce me to the wonders of kimchi: a wonderfully spicy pickled cabbage that went well with everything. Making kimchi for the first time is a bit of a worry, as it goes against most of the fundamental things we are taught about preserving anything – rather like the Thai habit of boiling coconut milk until it separates, it is just not how you expect to do something. Take heart, though, because the end result is not only delicious but healthy too. Try it with any rice dishes.

4 tbsp sea salt

500 g/1 lb. 2 oz. Chinese cabbage or pak choi, chopped into 2.5-cm/ 1-inch slices

100 g/3½ oz. shallots, roughly chopped

½ daikon radish or 4 large red radishes, quartered lengthways and cut into 1-cm/½-inch chunks

4 garlic cloves, crushed

5-cm/2-inch piece fresh ginger, peeled and grated

3 spring onions/scallions, very finely chopped

1 tbsp dried chilli/hot red pepper flakes

1 tbsp dried Japanese kelp/seaweed (optional)

500-ml/2-cup kilner-style jar with non-reactive lid

Pour 1 litre/4 cups water into a bowl, add the salt and stir until the salt has dissolved. This is the brine.

Put the cabbage, shallots and radish in a large bowl and cover with the brine. Cover and leave overnight in the fridge.

The next day, put the garlic in a mortar with the ginger, spring onions/ scallions and chilli flakes. Pound with a pestle to make a paste. Add the seaweed, if using. Drain the vegetables and return them to the large bowl. If the vegetables taste excessively salty, rinse them once with cold water and return them to the bowl. Add the garlic paste and mix thoroughly with the vegetables, ensuring that everything is coated.

Pack this mixture tightly into the kilner-style jar. Ideally, Kimchi ferments under pressure, so if you can find a suitable tea cup or bowl that can be put on top of the vegetable mixture to compress it when the lid is closed, this would be ideal. Place in a cool spot, but not the fridge, for 3–4 days. It is a good idea to open the jar daily and give the mixture a stir before resealing. This avoids the build up of pressure in the sealed container as the vegetables ferment and ensures everything is well coated throughout the process.

The kimchi is ready when the mixture tastes a little sour and the cabbage has begun to soften and look translucent. At this point remove the cup, seal the jar and transfer to the fridge. This will halt the fermentation process. Serve by draining the water and bringing the kimchi to room temperature.

Hot tip: Use this as a fantastic addition to any rice dish. It can be drizzled with a little sesame oil to serve. It will keep well in the fridge and is past its best when it begins to smell sweet or vaguely alcoholic.

RED CHILLI OIL *(opposite, right)*

This is a classic Chinese ingredient, an integral part of Szechuan cooking and the perfect accompaniment to pork wontons. It is hot, and it gets hotter the longer it is stored. Great modifications include reducing the chilli and adding a few bruised garlic cloves.

500 ml/2 cups vegetable oil or groundnut oil (avoid olive oil or strongly flavoured oils)

2 spring onions/scallions, bruised with the back of a knife

a thumb-sized piece fresh ginger, bruised with the back of a heavy knife or rolling pin

100 g/3½ oz. dried chilli/hot red pepper flakes

2 tsp Szechuan peppercorns

2 star anise

Heat the oil, onions and ginger in a medium saucepan over medium-high heat until the oil just begins to smoke. Remove from the heat and remove the onions from the oil. Set aside to cool a little.

Put the chilli flakes, peppercorns and star anise in medium ceramic bowl. Remove the ginger from the oil and pour the still-hot oil into the bowl. With a metal/ceramic spoon, give everything a good mix. Leave overnight for the flavours to infuse. The chilli, star anise and peppercorns should settle to the bottom of the bowl. Carefully pour the oil into a sterilized bottle, being careful not to disturb the sediment in the bottom of the bowl. I often strain the oil through a funnel lined with coffee filter paper to be sure to get all the oil and none of the flavouring ingredients. Seal tightly and store in a cool dark place for several months.

Hot tip: This is a fragrant oil for use in cooking and dressings. Use this to make Szechuan dipping sauce or to spice up noodles.

SZECHUAN RED & BLACK DIPPING SAUCE *(opposite, left)*

This is a lovely way to use your homemade Red Chilli Oil. It is worth trying to find black vinegar for this recipe; it is a fragrant, slightly alcoholic rice vinegar that adds an indefinable oriental quality to dishes.

2 tbsp Red Chilli Oil (see left)

1 tbsp Chinese black vinegar (Chinkiang vinegar) or balsamic vinegar

3 tbsp soy sauce

½ tbsp sesame oil

½ tsp ground Szechuan pepper

½ tsp sugar

1 garlic clove, crushed

1 tbsp finely grated or shredded fresh ginger

1 spring onion/scallion, finely chopped

In a small bowl, mix the Red Chilli Oil, vinegar, soy sauce and sesame oil. Add the pepper and sugar and mix to dissolve the sugar. Add the remaining ingredients and stir through until everything is mixed evenly together. Set aside for an hour to allow the flavours to infuse.

Hot tip: Use this with prawn/shrimp dumplings, beef or chicken gyoza, or Szechuan wontons.

CHINESE PICKLED GREEN CHILLIES

This is another must-have kitchen staple. I would definitely encourage you to make your own pickled chillies, as they are so much nicer than storebought ones.

120 g/4 oz. bullet-style hot green chillies or Jalapeños, sliced

100 ml/scant ½ cup boiling water

250 ml/1 cup Shaoxing rice wine

1 tbsp sugar

1 tsp sea salt

4 Szechuan peppercorns

½ star anise

Put the chillies in a bowl and pour the boiling water over them. After about 30 seconds, drain the chillies. Lay them on some paper towels and pat dry.

Heat the vinegar in a small saucepan, add the sugar and salt and stir until dissolved. Heat until it just comes to the boil.

Put the chillies in a sterilized container with a tightly fitting lid along with the peppercorns and the star anise. Pour the hot vinegar solution into the jar, ensuring that the chillies are covered. Seal the jar and give a quick shake. Allow to cool. Leave for at least 1 week: the longer the better!

Hot tip: Use this as a perfect side dish for stir fries or noodle dishes.

HUNAN CHILLI SAUCE

The Hunan region of China is known for its intensely spicy cuisine. It is also a hugely important region in the production of chillies themselves. This sauce is extremely hot and is in fact as much a pickle as a sauce. It is used in numerous recipes from Hunan including the infamous fish head soup!

100 g/3½ oz. fresh hot red chillies, deseeded and chopped

1 small ripe pear, peeled, cored and roughly chopped

4 garlic cloves, crushed

5-cm/2-inch piece fresh ginger, peeled and very finely chopped

1–2 tsp sea salt

2 tbsp Shaoxing rice wine

Put all the ingredients in a blender or food processor and pulse until smooth but thick. Transfer to a bowl and leave for 10–15 minutes.

Check the seasoning (it will be very spicy!) and add more salt or vinegar as required. Spoon the mixture into a sterilized glass jar, pressing it down to pack it into the jar. Leave a space of about 3 cm/1¼ inches at the top of the jar. Top up the jar with a little more rice wine vinegar to ensure that the paste is entirely covered. Seal the jar and store somewhere moderately cool and dark for a minimum of 20 days after which the sauce will be ready to use – with great care!

Hot tip: Use this in any classic hot and sour Hunan dish.

SZECHUAN CHILLI PASTE

We wanted to try to represent the flavours of the region with this paste using the simplest selection of ingredients we could find; as a result we didn't even ferment broad/fava beans, much to my disappointment. Facing Heaven chillies are readily available from Chinese supermarkets and add a distinct quality to this paste that is worth the extra effort involved in finding them.

1 tbsp vegetable oil

1 tsp toasted sesame oil

5 garlic cloves, finely chopped

3-cm/1¼-inch piece fresh ginger, peeled and finely chopped

1 onion, finely chopped

3 hot red chillies, deseeded and finely sliced

3 Facing Heaven chillies, deseeded

2 vine-ripened tomatoes, finely chopped

3 tbsp Shaoxing rice wine

½ tsp Szechuan pepper, freshly ground

1 tsp sea salt

1 tbsp sugar

2 tbsp Shaoxing rice wine

Heat both varieties of oil in a wok over high heat and fry the garlic and ginger for a few moments, stirring continuously. Add the onion and fry for a further 1 minute. Add the chillies and tomatoes and cook for a further 1 minute, then add the vinegar. Reduce the heat and simmer for 5 minutes.

Add the pepper, salt, sugar and rice wine and simmer until the ingredients are all cooked. Blitz to a smooth purée with a blender, food processor or stick blender. Transfer the paste to an airtight container and allow to cool. Allow the flavours to mingle for about 48 hours before using.

Hot tip: Use this to add a little kick to any Chinese meal or to flavour simple rice and noodle dishes.

HUNAN-STYLE CHILLI & BLACK BEAN SAUCE

Again this recipe pays tribute to the Hunan love of HEAT. Traditionally it is always cooked by steaming; completely sealing the bowl using clingfilm/plastic wrap before foil is a great way of ensuring that none of the flavour escapes in the cooking process!

3 tbsp sunflower oil

4 garlic cloves, crushed

2 tbsp dried chilli/hot red pepper flakes (or more if you like things even hotter!)

2 tsp Shaoxing rice wine

1 tsp toasted sesame oil

1 tbsp fermented black beans, rinsed

a large pinch of sea salt

Put all the ingredients in a heatproof glass or ceramic bowl. Mix together thoroughly. Cover with a sheet of clingfilm/plastic wrap and then tightly with a sheet of foil.

Place a steamer over a pan of boiling water and set the sealed bowl in the steamer. Place the lid on the steamer – or if the bowl is too big, cover it with a couple of layers of foil. Allow to steam for about 45 minutes, regularly checking the water level and topping it up with boiling water if required. Remove from the heat and allow to cool.

Serve immediately or refrigerate until needed, then allow to come to room temperature before serving.

Hot tip: Use this in spicy prawn/shrimp or chicken dishes.

SZECHUAN CHICKEN MARINADE

Szechuan pepper is extremely interesting; although not hot, it has a distinct lemon aroma and can produce a somewhat strange tingly (sometimes numbing) sensation in the mouth.

1 tbsp vegetable oil

1 large onion, chopped

2 garlic cloves, chopped

3-cm/1¼-inch piece fresh ginger, peeled and chopped

½–1 Habanero chilli, deseeded and finely chopped

2 tbsp sugar

2 tbsp dark soy sauce

2 tbsp Shaoxing rice wine

2 tbsp rice vinegar or white wine vinegar

½ tsp black peppercorns, 1 tsp Szechuan pepper and ½ tsp sea salt, ground together with a mortar and pestle

water, as required

Heat the oil in a wok and fry the onion, garlic and ginger until softened. Transfer to a food processor with the chilli, sugar, soy sauce, rice wine and rice vinegar. Blend to a smooth paste, adding a little water if required.

Return the paste to the wok with the ground pepper mixture and gently heat. Stir and cook until it comes to the boil, then reduce the heat and gently simmer for about 5 minutes, adding water if the paste becomes too thick. It should have the consistency of a thin purée. Taste and season further if required.

Remove from the heat and allow to cool to room temperature. Allow your chosen meat to marinate in this for a minimum of 2 hours.

Hot tip: Use this with chicken or maybe even pheasant.

CHINESE CURRY SAUCE (AN ENGLISH TAKEOUT TREATMENT!)

2 tbsp vegetable oil

1 onion, finely chopped

3–4 garlic cloves, crushed

5-cm/2-inch piece fresh ginger, peeled and finely chopped (or ideally microplaned)

1 tbsp Malay Curry Powder (see page 111)

2 tbsp plain/all-purpose flour

½ tsp black peppercorns, finely ground

½ tsp paprika

½ tsp Chinese five-spice

1 tbsp oyster sauce

1 tsp light soy sauce

warm water, as required

a large pinch of sugar

sea salt, to taste

This is a recipe that you will either see as a travesty or a triumph. Either way, it is full of classic ingredients and makes a fantastic base for chicken curry. It shows its real versatility when allowed to thicken a little and used as a dip for proper British chip-shop chips/fries! Having grown up in London and the southwest England, the idea of curry sauce or any sauce with chips was frankly disturbing. But it has its place, and when you find that place the pleasure to be derived is enormous!

Heat the oil in a saucepan over medium heat. Gently fry the onion, stirring regularly, until it begins to soften. Add the garlic and ginger and fry for another couple of minutes.

Stir in the Malay Curry Powder and flour and fry for 2–3 minutes, stirring to stop the ingredients sticking to the pan. Now add the pepper, paprika, five-spice, oyster sauce and soy sauce. Continue cooking and mixing to make a thick paste. Gradually add warm water, stirring continuously to blend the water with the paste until you have a reached a thick gravy consistency.

Add the sugar and bring to the boil. Reduce the heat and simmer for about 3–5 minutes, allowing the sauce to thicken a little. Season to taste with salt.

Hot tip: Use this as a base for a Chinese chicken curry. Or let it thicken a little more when cooking and it is the perfect curry sauce for dipping chips/fries into!

JAPANESE CURRY POWDER

Since the days of the Raj, the British have taken it upon themselves to spread curry around the world with evangelical zeal and so it is only moderately surprising to learn that curry was first introduced to Japan in the late 19th century by the British. Even the Imperial Japanese Navy adopted curry as its favourite dish from the British Navy. Curry rice is now ubiquitous throughout Japan and is generally made using an instant curry roux. This spice recipe just needs to be fried with oil and flour to make just such a roux. Loosen with water and serve over plain steamed rice for an unexpected taste of modern Japan.

3 tbsp ground turmeric

2 tbsp ground coriander

1 tbsp ground cumin

1 tsp ground cardamom

1 tsp ground black pepper

½ tsp cayenne pepper

½ tsp ground fennel seeds

¼ tsp ground cloves

¼ tsp ground bay

a large pinch of grated nutmeg

a large pinch of ground cinnamon

2 dried sage leaves, rubbed to a powder

Put all the ingredients in a jar, shake to mix, then seal tightly. Store in a cool, dark place until required.

Hot tip: Use this mixed with oil and flour in a hot saucepan to make a classic Japanese curry sauce.

CHILLI PICKLED GINGER

Pickled ginger (and pickled garlic for that matter) are delights that you can only enjoy when you reach a certain age. However, once you embrace pickles there is no going back... that reminds me – pickled eggs!

250 g/9 oz. fresh ginger, avoiding any tough or dry, fibrous roots as much as possible

a kettle of boiling water

250 ml/1 cup Japanese rice vinegar

6 tbsp sugar

½ tbsp salt

5 medium-heat red bullet-style chillies, halved lengthways and deseeded

500-ml/2-cup kilner-style jar with non-reactive lid

Peel the ginger. Using a sharp knife (or mandoline if you have one), slice the ginger as thinly as you can. Put the sliced ginger in a large bowl and pour the boiling water over it. Give it a little stir. After about 30 seconds, drain it and lay the ginger slices on paper towels. Pat dry with more paper towels.

Pour the vinegar and sugar into a saucepan and bring to the boil over medium heat, stirring to dissolve the sugar. Add the salt and stir to dissolve. Now boil for about 30 seconds, then remove from the heat.

Put the ginger and chilli halves in the kilner-style jar. Pour over the vinegar solution, ensuring that the ginger and chillies are submerged. Seal the lid and allow to cool naturally. Store in a cool, dark place.

The ginger will be ready to eat in about 1 week but will keep quite happily in the fridge, even after opening, for 4–6 months.

Hot tip: Use this in salads and sandwiches, or on the side of any spicy dish.

TERIYAKI MARINADE

(opposite)

Teriyaki is in fact more of a way of cooking than a recipe; in that sense it's a bit like Indian tandoori. In Japanese 'yaki' means 'to grill/broil' (or sometimes 'roas') and 'teri' means 'sheen' or 'lustre'. So to cook something 'teriyaki' means to grill/broil it with a lustrous or glazed surface. The key ingredient in achieving this sheen is mirin. Mirin is a kind of low-alcohol 'sake'. The most authentic sort of mirin is 'hon' mirin; this literally translates as 'true' mirin and has an alcohol content of 14%. 'Shio' mirin is the other acceptable rice wine to use in teriyaki; it too contains alcohol but has salt added. This makes it undrinkable as wine and thus avoids the duty levied on alcohol!

1.5-cm/½-inch piece fresh ginger, peeled and finely grated, preferably microplaned	1 small garlic clove, crushed
	3 tbsp Tamari soy sauce
	2 tbsp 'hon' mirin
1 Shishito chilli, deseeded and very finely chopped	1 tbsp rice vinegar
	2 tsp honey or brown sugar

Put the ginger, chilli and garlic into a mortar and pound with a pestle to a smooth paste. Add the liquid ingredients and blend together until everything is evenly mixed.

Hot tip: Use this with chicken or salmon.

JAPANESE PICKLED GINGER SALAD DRESSING

You get a lovely hint of warmth from the homemade Chilli Pickled Ginger in this recipe. Do not limit this salad dressing to just Asian dishes – it is lovely over any kind of chicken salad and almost perfect with a finely chopped Russian salad of tuna, carrots, peas, potato, parsley and capers.

1 small onion, finely chopped	2 tsp sugar
	½ tsp ground black pepper
1 carrot, finely chopped	2 tsp toasted sesame seeds
3 tbsp soy sauce	3 tbsp groundnut oil
2 tbsp Japanese rice vinegar	
1 tbsp finely chopped Chilli Pickled Ginger (see page 123)	

Put the onion, carrot, soy sauce, vinegar, Chilli Pickled Ginger, sugar, pepper and sesame seeds in a food processor or blender and blend to a smooth paste. Continue to blend while gradually adding the oil so that the mixture emulsifies. Serve immediately.

Hot tip: Use this as a dressing for a simple salad of gem lettuce, hard-boiled eggs and grated carrot.

INDEX

ACKNOWLEDGEMENTS

When I wrote this for *The Red Hot Chilli Cookbook* I utterly failed to mention a great many people without whom the whole project would have been a disaster – so this time I am apologizing in advance to those I forget.

Becky, Freddie, Theo, Ella and Monty for accepting that they have a slightly distracted husband and father, and encouraging me to carry on anyway. Sam, who despite working with me for 6 years unbelievably still supports these 'new ideas'. My editor Céline for patiently dealing with all the headaches my sporadic way of working creates without shouting at me once. Colin and Linda for not complaining that every meal contains chilli.

Owen and Michelle, Patrick and Katharina, Tim and Athene, Geoff and Liz, Anna, Chris and Rachael, Tony and Linda, Jamie and all their children for being the people who I love to experiment on. Cindy, Julia, Leslie, Lauren and everyone else at RPS who again made this fun! Peter and Lizzy for (again) making my recipes look stunning. And a few people who inspired me to write about food: Elizabeth David, Keith Floyd, Rick Stein, Simon Majumdar, Hugh F-W, Kenny Atkinson, and finally my Mum who, despite everything, ensured I knew how to cook and my Dad who always ate everything I made for him.

ABOUT THE AUTHOR

Dan May's love of music and lack of a better idea led him to start his working life touring some of the least pleasant venues in Britain and Europe in various bands before a brief stint working as a lighting engineer was ended by a St Patrick's Day incident involving Guinness, a very high lighting rig and cavalier approach to risk assessment. For the next 13 years Dan travelled and worked as a landscape photographer, producing images that were used by companies all over the world. Visiting some of the most remote places in the world brought him into close contact with chillies, and a relationship developed that was unintentionally life-changing.

Dan grew some chillies as a hobby in 2005 and before he knew it he had the world's most northerly chilli farm and had accidentally changed career (again). He developed Trees Can't Dance, his idiosyncratic chilli brand and ended up supplying sauces, pastes and marinades to everyone from multiple supermarkets to local stores both in the UK and abroad. He still grows a lot of chillies and spices and spends most of each day trying to work on new and exciting ways to use them.

Always ready with an opinion, Dan is frequently quoted in national press with regard to the latest trends in food and chillies. He has also appeared on Radio 2 as the chilli guru for Chris Evans and Simon Mayo.